MW00623142

SLAYING

THE

GORGON

THE RISE OF THE
STORYTELLING
INDUSTRIAL COMPLEX

To Debora,
A pleasure meeting
you. Good luck with
your Storytelling.
Joe McH

JOE McHUGH

Calling
Crane

Calling Crane Publishing
www.callingcrane.com
© 2013 Joe McHugh

Printed in the United States of America

This book is dedicated to
Utah Phillips, friend and mentor

CONTENTS

"*At times one has to deal with hidden enemies, intangible influences that slink into dark corners and from this hiding affect people by suggestion. In instances like this, it is necessary to trace these things back to the most secret recesses, in order to determine the nature of the influences to be dealt with . . . The very anonymity of such plotting requires an especially vigorous and indefatigable effort, but this is worthwhile. For when such elusive influences are brought into the light and branded, they lose their power over people.*"

—from the *I-Ching* translated by Richard Wilheim, Princeton University Press

INTRODUCTION

The Wave That Eats People

ON A SMALL ISLAND OFF THE COAST of Thailand there lives a community of fisher people known as the Morgan Sea Gypsies. Since time out of mind they have gathered around their campfires at night to tell the story of the Laboon, the great wave that eats people. So fierce is the Laboon, in fact, that the other waves are afraid of it and run away before it arrives. Thus the story counsels the people to seek the safety of higher ground whenever the waves flee because it means the angry Laboon is on its way.

And this is exactly what the Sea Gypsies did just before the 2004 tsunami struck their remote island. Tragically, on far too many other Indonesian and Thai beaches, people ventured out onto the sand exposed by the receding waves to take photographs or pick up stranded fish and were killed when the great wave washed ashore.

But not the Sea Gypsies. All one hundred and eighty-one men, women, and children on Surin Island survived because they fled to a temple high up in the mountains, heeding the story of the Laboon, a legend that had been faithfully passed down from generation to generation.

* * *

I begin with the story of the Morgan Sea Gypsies because storytelling in its most basic form is about survival. It is about our physical and psychological survival, a way of making sense of the world. We use stories to pass on what we've learned, to lift and strengthen our spirits, and to remind ourselves of the common origin of all humankind.

But we can also use stories for mischief, to confuse and deceive, to turn one group of people against another, and to sap the joy and hope out of life. Thus there is both promise and peril in this uniquely human activity; storytellers can serve us, but they can also harm us.

By exploring the art and practice of storytelling in the modern world and its relationship to the human mind, this book provides a framework for understanding the significant changes taking place in the realms of politics, religion, public education, and culture.

- What causes the political gridlock that prevents us from solving the problems that threaten our very survival?
- Why are movie actors, professional wrestlers, and comedians becoming governors and United States senators?
- Why is the judge of a reality television show paid two hundred times more than a justice of the U.S. Supreme Court?
- Why does public education's reliance on standardized testing cause some school officials and teachers to falsify test scores?
- Why are churches holding worship services in movie theaters?

- How did a spat over a microphone in 1980 change the course of world history?
- And last, what is a "sustainable imagination," and what happens when a society industrializes the way it tells its stories?

These are some of the questions we wrestle with and it can feel as if a tsunami of discontent and ill will is sweeping over us, a Laboon that will devour all that we hold dear.

For the past thirty-five years I have made my living as a traditional storyteller. I've spun yarns at festivals and colleges, museums and libraries, on television and by the light of a crackling campfire on the riverbank after a day of whitewater rafting. I've even told ghost stories deep inside a coal mine on Halloween. It's been a traveler's life with its share of uncertainty but also moments of wonder and a wealth of opportunities to make friends. I particularly enjoy telling stories to young people. I tell them how Jack climbed a mountain to defeat the ugly old giant and save the king's daughter or how a wizard turned an old woman into a woodpecker because she was too nosy. Then again I might tell them how Davy Crockett could grin the bark off a tree or why some snakes have rattles at the end of their tails.

Lately, however, I have been telling a different kind of story: a story for adults. And like those I tell children, it is a tale filled with giants and ogres, evil spellcasters and snaked-haired monsters, magical wands and enchanted mirrors. Only I'm not telling about "once upon a time in a land far away" but about what is happening in our own world today. Let me explain.

In the early 1990s, my wife Paula and I were experimenting with ways to enliven the learning experience for young people in the classroom. One approach was to have students perform radio plays, which led the California Department of Education to ask us to design a tobacco-use prevention curriculum for elementary schools that would include a recording of a professionally performed radio play, information on the history and health impacts of tobacco use, and a do-it-yourself radio drama script with instructions on how to make the necessary sound effects. It took us a number of months to complete the project, and, during that time, I researched how tobacco companies marketed their products to young people. Not only did I find that some of the companies employed cartoon characters like Joe Camel to grab the attention of young consumers, but they also paid large sums of money to film studios to include pro-tobacco messages in major films. The Disney Corporation's 1989 film *Honey I Shrunk the Kids*, for instance, included a scene designed to convince the viewer that tobacco wasn't addictive, but that someone, in this case the caring, worried father of the lead teenage male heartthrob, only smoked when he was worried, giving the impression that a person could *choose* to smoke or not whenever he wanted. Other films at the time with pro-tobacco messages included *Lethal Weapon* and *Superman II*.

It's fair to say that analyzing tobacco ads, reading tobacco company internal memos, and watching tobacco-friendly feature films politicized my thinking about the role of storytelling and media in our lives. Soon afterward, I began working with troubled youths in juvenile detention facilities and treatment centers. The more I worked with these young people, the more I saw how mass media shaped their view of the world and influenced their often destructive behaviors. Blatant cynicism, gratuitous violence, and degrading sexual attitudes were increasingly the norm and not the exception in youth entertainment. The intention of these stories as I saw it was not to pass on wisdom, like the tale of the Laboon, but rather to shock, offend, confound, and in many cases bring about, as the director Wes Craven states while playing himself in one of his own films, "the death of innocence."

All this made me both sad and angry because I was raising my own children and did not want them exposed to these dehumanizing influences. But if so many kids loved going to these movies, watching these television shows, and playing these video games, and if their parents didn't seem to mind, who was I to complain or raise a rumpus? I wasn't a politician, a child psychologist, or a professional media critic. No one elected me the nation's culture tsar. Quite the opposite. I was wary of those who only too eagerly set themselves up as the Morality Police. Nor was I a supporter of artistic censorship.

But I began to see that as a working storyteller, I might have a responsibility to speak out in the same way a surgeon would if he discovered that the scalpels were improperly sterilized in the OR, or an architect who, while visiting a building site, notices the contractor has substituted substandard materials for those called for in the plans. Even if the building isn't one of his own, he still has an ethical responsibility to raise the alarm because he *knows* the building is unsafe and could collapse. Well, my expertise was storytelling and I believed I saw things in the way stories were structured and told that were hidden from most non-storytellers. When the man behind the curtain, in other words, turned a wheel or pushed a lever, I knew what the wheel and lever actually *did*. So as the months slipped by, I became increasingly burdened by this question of my responsibility.

Then one day I was asked to give a keynote address at a national conference for juvenile court judges. Lacking what I considered the necessary academic or celebrity credentials, I was at first intimidated by the request until the conference organizer, a lovely man named Jim Toner, convinced me that the judges genuinely wanted to hear my views regarding the impact of the entertainment industry on young people. Thus inspired, I created a presentation titled *Cinderella Meets Freddy Krueger: Storytelling in Modern America* that combined projected still images, segments of recorded audio, and several clips from popular feature films. I compared a traditional ghost story— in most versions of the Cinderella story, it is the ghost of the mother, not a fairy godmother, who returns to aid her ill-used daughter—with the new breed of ghost/demon stories coming out of Hollywood. I hoped to show how the structure of narrative itself was being radically altered from one celebrating the victory of good over evil and a universe responsive to our actions, into one in which people are adrift in a chaotic and meaningless universe, where a person's fate is determined not by his moral or ethical behavior or acts of kindness but by chance, a mere toss of the dice. Walk in the wrong door at the wrong time and you risk being slashed to pieces by a knife-wielding maniac. End of story.

But whether the universe is ordered and beneficent or random and cruel was not the question I wanted to put before the judges. After all, that is a matter of opinion. Instead, I wanted to explore why our primary organs of storytelling— companies like Viacom, Miramax, FOX, Time-Warner—were giving up on the traditional structure of narrative, one that has come down to us from earlier times when, ironically, life must have seemed a great deal more random and cruel than it does for suburban kids today.

So the day of the conference arrived and I gave my keynote. Afterward, a number of the judges told me that my use of folklore motifs and personal anecdotes in particular had helped clarify many of the troubling attitudes and behaviors they confronted in their courtrooms every day. I was asked to speak at other juvenile justice conferences but I sensed that I was missing something, something important. I therefore decided to interview other working storytellers: filmmakers, visual effects artists, talk show hosts, preachers, courtroom attorneys, playwrights, poets, journalists—anyone who could help me better understand what was going on. One storyteller recommended the book *Understanding Media, the Extensions of Man* by the noted Canadian scholar Marshall McLuhan. As I read McLuhan, I was captivated by his theory that the *medium* of storytelling does more to shape people's beliefs and behaviors than the *content* of the stories. Hitherto, I had focused on the influence of content and the sophisticated corporate money machines that decide which particular content gets foisted on our young people through the "mainstream" media. I began to investigate the electronic mediums of storytelling, and, as I did so, I saw how the impact of these new mediums spread far beyond the precincts of youth entertainment, reaching into nearly every aspect of our personal and collective lives. Other authors whose works contributed to my understanding of this phenomena included Neil Postman, Leonard Shlain, Walter Ong, and the historian Karen Armstrong.

In time, I changed the name of my presentation to *Slaying the Gorgon: the Rise of the Storytelling Industrial Complex*, because I saw in the myth of Perseus and Medusa a unique way of understanding how storytelling mediums influence society.

As a child, the first thing I did when my copy of *Highlights* magazine arrived in the mail was turn to the hidden pictures page where I would eagerly search for the spoon in the branches of a tree, the garden hoe in the picket fence, and the face of an old man in the clouds. This, I think, is the best way to grapple with the hurly-burly of modern media. We begin seeing only what is on the surface: a four-star general is fired because of an unguarded remark made to a reporter from a rock music magazine, a candidate accepts his party's nomination for president inside a football stadium, a movie star protests the government's foreign policy by getting arrested, a preacher is elected governor and then given his own television talk show, and a poster artist convinces people to occupy a city park. But if we are patient and sufficiently inquisitive, we begin see the hidden pictures beneath the activity and apparent confusion. We see the recurring patterns, the power deals between warlords and mythmakers, the age-old conflict between what I call *mythos* knowing and *logos* knowing. All the same, I think we should avoid trying to be too up-to-the-minute in our observations. Instead, I recommend that we take advantage of the distance of time for it is easier to map the shape of a coastline or an approaching hurricane through the lens of a camera on an orbiting satellite rather than by standing on the shore where vision is obstructed by sand dunes, boardwalks, and summer cottages. That's how I found those hidden objects in my Highlights magazine, not by bringing the page up close to my nose but by holding it out at arm's length and squinting.

And as for the current popularity of social networking mediums such as Facebook and Twitter, I know there are people who claim these mediums are turning human storytelling on its head. In the long term, they may be right although I have my doubts—we've been at this storytelling business since we huddled together in caves and micro bursts of text or the corralling of snippets of personal information with a photograph or two, even a short video, does not necessarily a story or storyteller make. Therefore, I will leave this topic, along with the latest political upset and celebrity scandal, for other culture watchers to ponder in the hope that the frameworks and ideas presented in this book will suffice in providing the reader with a foundational understanding of how we seek to communicate the essential truths of life with each other and with those who will come after us.

* * *

I conclude this introduction the same way I started, with a story. Some years ago Paula and I directed a summer camping program for young people called *Camp ImaginAction*, a week-long language-arts camp held in the High Sierra of northern California. Each night we gathered around a campfire and told stories and sang songs, after which the counselors would lead their young charges back to their tents in the dark to read them stories from American literature, the soft glow of their flashlights shimmering like fairy orbs upon the canvas of each tent. And the fun continued the next day as the campers participated in activities inspired by the late-night stories. They built *Huckleberry Finn* rafts and learned how to work with sled dogs like the mushers in Jack London's novel *Call of the Wild*.

Even the start of camp was designed to impress upon the campers the fact that for the next six days and nights they were going to be active participants in the telling of stories, no longer passive consumers. That's why a few days before driving up to the camp we stopped by the local Salvation Army store and picked up a rather large console TV, the kind I grew up with in the 1960s.

Shortly after the campers arrived, we loaded the television onto a sled-style gurney, draped it with flowers, and in the manner of a funeral procession, marched everyone through the ponderosa pine forest to where we had dug a grave. Three of our number were counselors who, dressed in black, sniffled into their handkerchiefs remembering what a good and loyal companion the television had been while I assured the campers that we weren't burying every television set, just this one because it had died from overuse.

When we reached the gravesite I cut the power cord and handed it to one of the bereaved counselors as another played taps on the camp bugle. While we had to struggle to keep from laughing the campers were as serious as drenched cats. Why had the television died? they asked a second and third time.

Because it wore out, I told them.

They asked if we'd come back later and dig it up and get it fixed.

No, I said. We would let it rest in peace. And for the rest of the week we would live and tell our own stories.

The campers were quiet as we lowered the television into the ground and they lined up single file so each could throw a handful of dirt on top of it. When everyone had had their turn, three other counselors and I began shoveling the displaced dirt back into the hole. I hadn't, however, realized how long this would take. So after a few awkward minutes during which the campers stood around with nothing to do, I asked Paula to take everyone to the fire pit for the first evening campfire.

One young boy of ten or eleven, however, asked if he might stay behind and help bury the television. I chalked this up to an attraction to shovels and dirt and men working together and I said "Sure" and handed him a shovel. To be honest, with seventy-five campers to entertain, feed, and see off safely to bed, I paid the boy scant attention until I noticed that he was shoveling as though his life depended on it and muttering to himself, not unlike a Tibetan monk chanting his mantra. As I inched closer to make out what he was saying, this was what I heard with each scoop of dirt that fell on top of the television:

"Now my brother will play with me. Now my brother will play with me. Now my brother will play with me."

It is to that boy that I dedicate this book.

CHAPTER 1

The Enchanted Mirror

THE GREEK LEGEND OF PERSEUS AND MEDUSA offers us a unique insight into why human beings tell stories. Perseus was the child of Zeus and a mortal named Danae. While living on the island of Serifos, Perseus attended a banquet hosted by King Polydectes who had lecherous designs on Perseus' mother and wanted the young hero out of the way. To achieve this end, he tricked Perseus into vowing that he would slay the gorgon Medusa, a terrible monster who had laid waste to the countryside.

According to the Roman author Ovid, Medusa was once a proud and beautiful woman, but the goddess Athena turned her into a gorgon after finding Medusa in the arms of her lover Poseidon. Gorgons were golden-winged creatures with writhing, sharp-fanged snakes for hair, curved boar-like tusks for teeth, and razor-keen bronze talons for hands. Whoever gazed upon a gorgon was instantly turned to stone. No match for such a terrible foe, Perseus was confronted with a seemingly impossible task: how could he cut off the gorgon's head without being turned to stone? So Perseus prayed to Athena, the goddess of wisdom, who came to him and told him to polish his bronze shield until it shone like a mirror.[1]

"Use Medusa's reflection in the shield to guide your sword," the goddess instructed him. "That way you will not be turned to stone."

By following this advice, Perseus was able to complete his quest and return to Serifos carrying the gorgon's head in a magic leather satchel. Upon entering Polydectes' palace, Perseus took revenge upon the cruel king. Averting his eyes and warning his mother to do the same, Perseus pulled the hideous severed head from the satchel and turned Polydectes and his court into cold, lifeless heaps of stone.

Despite being thousands of years old, this tale speaks to our current day predicament. In the symbolic language of legend, Medusa is Reality, and the nature of Reality is paradox.

Have you ever noticed that no matter how hard you try to do something right and good something always seems to go wrong? You might achieve your aims but inevitably there's a downside, an unexpected and unwanted consequence that springs from your well-intended actions. Let's say you're the chairman of the planning board for your town, and Walmart wants to build a big box store. Some people in your town are struggling financially and would benefit from the lower prices that Walmart offers, not to mention the jobs. But you also fear that Walmart will change the character of the town and drive local retailers out of business, the same retailers who for years

---

1. According to the Greeks, there were three gorgons who were sisters. After Perseus slayed Medusa, her two sisters chased him through the air beating their powerful golden wings while Perseus fled before them wearing the winged sandals the god Hermes had given him. Eventually, Perseus threw off his pursuers and even managed to rescue the beautiful Andromeda from a sea monster before returning home to Serifos.

have paid taxes and supported little league teams and food bank drives. You're damned if you do and damned if you don't.

Then there are the great paradoxes: you live, you strive, you love, you sacrifice, and then you die as if it was all for nothing. If you are religious and believe God is all good, all knowing, and omnipresent, then why is there evil, cruelty, and suffering in the world?

So the ancient Greeks gave us the gorgon Medusa, a richly imagined physical representation of paradoxical Reality. She gnashes her terrible teeth as anxious serpents hiss and writhe about her head. Global warming, immigration reform, abortion, the war in Afghanistan, civil liberties versus national security; these are all enormous, ugly gorgons. And the more determined we are to remain intellectually honest with ourselves, the greater the risk that we reach a point when we throw up our hands in despair and say, "Why the hell even try?"

We've looked upon the gorgon, wrestled with the conflicted choices offered by Reality, and been effectively turned to stone. Medusa has robbed us of the ability to act with any degree of confidence or joy. This I believe is what people fear most, this being turned to stone, and they will do almost anything to avoid it.

Which brings us to the part of the legend when Athena tells Perseus to polish his shield so that it shines like a mirror. The mirror symbolizes myth, which is expressed through story, image, and ritual. Myth is not Reality; it is only a reflection of Reality. A true mythic story may be entertaining, an opportunity to laugh or shed a tear, but its primary function is to empower people to act with decisiveness and a sense of meaning. In other words, by allowing the mythic story inside the mirror to guide his actions, a person can slay the gorgon and not be turned to stone.

This then raises the question: who are today's storytellers, the mythmakers who polish and hold up the mirrors for the rest of us to look at?

Some are individuals with names like Oprah, O'Reilly, Scorsese, and Spielberg, while others are corporations with names like Paramount, New York Times, Disney, NBC, Home Box Office, CNN, and Random House.

Some of these individuals and corporations take their responsibilities seriously and try to hold up mirrors that reflect Reality as accurately as possible, while others hold up wildly distorted, fun house mirrors.

In either case, what people crave is simplicity, not paradox. Reduce it down to basics, they demand: tell me what to do, where to shop, and who to vote for. But whatever you do, keep me from looking at that angry gal having the bad hair day.

And not surprisingly, our modern-day mythmakers are only too happy to oblige.

"The monster Medusa was slain today by a daring youth named Perseus. Details at eleven!"

The mythmakers take their soft cloths—camera lens filters and digital audio compressors, computer-generated graphics and prerecorded laugh tracks—and they rub and rub the bronze shield until the stories fairly fly off the mirrored surface. These twenty-first century storytellers use their electronic mirrors to tell people what they want to hear: "You're a ditto-head, a patriot, a red-blooded, gun-owning American," or "You're a faithful friend of the Earth, champion of the underdog, a *Yes We Can* kind of person," or "You're one of God's own chosen and will be raptured in the End Times," or "You're a true, dyed-in-the-wool, tailgating fan of (fill in the appropriate name: Fighting Irish, Tar Heels, the Dodgers) and when your team wins, you win. Hurrah!"

The list of mirror messages is long and predictable, because each tribe of humankind has its own mythic narrative, a core-animating story that determines the group's beliefs and behaviors, and electronic media has become a mechanism for delivering those stories. Furthermore, because of improvements in communication technologies and the evolution of the corporation as a social and economic structure, media companies have become masters at providing these myths, and, by so doing, they have acquired significant influence over almost every aspect of our lives.

CHAPTER 2

Mythos versus Logos

TO BETTER UNDERSTAND THE MEDIA, we need to examine how human beings actually perceive the world. It's said that there are two kinds of people in the world: those who think there are two kinds of people, and the rest who don't. I take a similar dualistic approach when considering the nature of human consciousness. As I see it, there are basically two ways of knowing the world. One I call "*mythos*" knowing and the other I call "*logos*" knowing. *Mythos* knowing comes from experiencing the world through our five physical senses: sight, sound, smell, taste, and touch. It also includes those other forms of sensation we call intuition, state of grace, love-at-first-sight, and premonition. All are forms of sensory perception and constitute *mythos* knowing.[2]

2. A clarification concerning word usage: *mythos* and *logos* are wonderful, intriguing words. *Mythos* is most often used to describe the complex values and attitudes of a particular people as expressed through their myths and legends. The Greek word *logos* traditionally means word, thought, or principle. Philosophers and theologians also use *logos* when referring to human reason, rationality, and divine reason, which some believe has existed unchanged since the origins of the cosmos. In an effort, however, to simplify the way we talk about the dual nature of human consciousness and how the mediums of storytelling shape those two forms of knowing, I decided to repurpose these words for use within this context. Of course, anyone altering the meaning of words runs the

Logos knowing, by contrast, arises from this neat trick we've learned to do with our primate brains, which is to think abstractly, to break down the world into its component parts, which can then be measured, arranged, and categorized. *Logos* knowing also converts spoken language into a series of seemingly meaningless slashes and squiggles of ink on paper or patterns of pixels that we call "letters" and "numbers." We string together these squiggles to create words and amounts, sentences and equations, literature and mathematics. You're looking at those slashes and squiggles now.[3]

Logos knowing also divides time into discreet units called seconds, minutes, hours, and days, and physical space into feet, yards, miles, and acres.

As forms of consciousness, *mythos* and *logos* knowing are both complementary and oppositional. *Mythos* knowing is the knowing of the artist and mystic, while *logos* knowing is the knowing of the scientist, engineer, lawyer, and corporate manager.

Mythos knowing inside the brain is concrete: a tree is a tree, a can of spinach is a can of spinach—or as Popeye the Sailor might say, "They is what they is." Objects, therefore, are not representations of something else as is the case with *logos* knowing, which employs an elaborate system of visual symbols that have in themselves no relationship with any object, action, or feeling in the physical world. When you see the letter C on

---

risk of generating more confusion than understanding, but I don't believe this will be a problem in the case of mythos and logos, because they seem able to encompass these new meanings quite well.

3. In English, written and printed letters are used to indicate the specific sounds of spoken language. Other languages such as Chinese and Japanese are translated into text using a sophisticated system of symbols with each indicating a specific object or action rather than the sound of the word.

a page, for instance, you don't think of anything else. It's just a pleasant half-circle of ink on the paper.

Now add an A so that you have CA.

Now a T and you have CAT.

The image of an animal pops into your head.

But now add a W—CATW

How very confusing! What the heck is a CATW?

Then another A—CATWA

Then the letter L—CATWAL

And finally a K.

Ah-hah!

Now you have CATWALK and the image of an animal is gone and in its place is something very different.

That is how *logos* knowing works. And notice the amount of time it took your eye to make the journey from one letter to the next, moving from left to right across the page, as your brain converted the symbols into meaning. You first envisioned a small animal and then a narrow elevated walkway. It felt as if this transformation occurred instantaneously but in fact it took time, if only a split second. And it takes more time to add more letters, which become words, then sentences, then paragraphs, which the brain converts into even more meaning.

"The catwalk . . . listen . . . do you hear footsteps?" Bill whispers to Margo as he slides the cold steel .38 snub-nose Smith & Wesson from its holster. "I think the murderer is coming this way. When I shout, turn on the lights."

This experience of sequential time is a trait of *logos* knowing, whereas *mythos* knowing tends to concern itself with the present moment, the here and now, because that's the source of all sensations. History as a field of study begins with the invention of writing, and the very experience of time as being linear with one event causing the next is an integral part of *logos* knowing.

To the *mythos* knowing part of the brain, the memories of events as they recede into the past quickly take on the nature of legend rather than experienced fact. This holds true for the Trojan Wars as it does for the family story about your great-great-grandfather's friendship with Davy Crockett. Conversely, *logos* knowing strives for the experience of historic certitude and does this by placing events like markers along a continuum, what we call a timeline.

The fact that the brain is divided equally into two hemispheres called the cerebral cortices may indicate the mind's propensity to divide itself into two ways of knowing. Noted Harvard-trained brain scientist Jill Bolte Taylor described the functioning of each hemisphere of the brain in her TED lecture about her experience of having a stroke:

"Our right hemisphere thinks in pictures and it learns kinesthetically through the movement of our bodies. Information, in the form of energy, streams in simultaneously through all of our sensory systems and then it explodes into this enormous collage of what this present moment looks like, what this present moment smells like and tastes like, what it feels like and what it sounds like . . . Our left hemisphere is a very different place. [It] thinks linearly and methodically. Our left hemisphere is all about the past and it's all about the future. Our left hemisphere is designed to take that enormous collage of the present moment and start picking out details—details and more details about those details. It then categorizes and organizes all that information, associates it with everything in the past we've ever learned, and projects into the future all of our possibilities. And our left hemisphere thinks in language. It's that ongoing brain chatter that connects me and my internal world to my external world. It's that little voice that says to me, 'Hey, you've got to remember to pick up bananas on your way home. I need them in the morning.'"

Of course, we hardly ever use just one hemisphere of our brain—there's a lot of electrical activity going back and forth between the hemispheres thanks to the three hundred million axonal fibers of the corpus callosum. By the same token, we rarely use just one way of knowing—there is usually a degree of blending.

Spoken language can be regarded as an abstract system of sounds that relies on *logos* knowing to function in ways similar to written language. An audible expression that linguists call the "signifier" relates to an object, action, or sensation called the "signified." So if I say the word "couch," you conjure up in your mind the image of a large piece of furniture in your living room where people sit. The same process takes place when you *read* the word "couch;" that's your *logos* knowing kicking into gear. But spoken language adds the physical sensation of sound, which also activates the *mythos*-knowing region of the brain. My voice may be pleasant or annoying, soothing or grating. Besides communicating the signifiers of language, each voice has its unique timbre, rhythm, and modulation. Some individuals can move large numbers of people solely by the sensations their voices induce in their listeners. Think, for instance, of Barack Obama, Martin Luther King, Garrison Keillor, Ronald Reagan, and Susan Stamberg. And for my money, no narrator could top Boris Karloff when it came to bringing the story of *Peter and the Wolf* to life.

When spoken language marries music it appeals more deeply to our *mythos* knowing. There are gifted performers who can sing a simple lyric such as, "Baby, baby, please don't go," and sell a million CDs.

Thus spoken language is a bridge between *logos* and *mythos* knowing. The object I see in my mind when I say the word "couch" is old-fashioned with large rounded arms and puffy brown cushions, while the couch you see in your mind is sleek and modern. We have communicated but not completely. I would need to use more words to get you to see the old-fashioned couch I'm picturing. Or if we were sitting across from each other I could add physical gestures to my words. Or I could show you a photograph of a couch in a magazine. We would now be in the realm of *mythos* knowing. The photograph is still a signifier, a stand-in for the real object—you can't take a Sunday afternoon nap on a photograph—but the image is much closer to physical reality and therefore more active in the *mythos*-knowing part of our brains.

As I said, m*ythos* and *logos* knowing rarely function in isolation.

Here's a simple exercise to help us distinguish *mythos* knowing from *logos* knowing. Imagine for a moment that you are a first-time visitor to New York City. You have the day to yourself and as you stroll down Broadway through Times Square, pedestrians, cars, and store windows full of electronic gear and designer luggage compete for your attention with larger-than-life images of supermodels and product trademarks flashing across billboards on the sides of buildings. Your ears are filled with the honking of taxicabs and the rumble of airplanes overhead. You are drawn by the aromas wafting from a street vendor's cart and you purchase a hot dog that you smear with tangy mustard and devour as you continue on your way, the sunlight warming your face, a light breeze lifting your hair.

Or perhaps you're walking through the woods in the Blue Ridge Mountains of Virginia. It's early November and songbirds flit from tree to tree overhead as you kick through a carpet of newly fallen leaves, all red and gold. You come upon a stream where two fishermen cast their shimmering lines through the autumn air to fall upon the water that gurgles over worn rocks.

You smell the rich damp earth as you pick and chew a sprig of wild peppermint, the taste dancing on your tongue. You kneel and trail your fingers through the crisp, cold water. In both these situations, the *mythos*-knowing part of your brain is in charge. Not only are you attending to an assortment of pleasant physical sensations, but your sense of time also ebbs and flows, expands and contracts. You are caught up in the varied tempos of life as they happen around you.

Now let's re-imagine the two situations: You are in the Big Apple to meet with a new literary agent. You have never been to her office; you've only talked to her on the telephone. As you hurry down the street, you scan the doorways of buildings for street numbers. You are running late because you took the wrong subway, the local instead of the express, and you keep glancing at your cell phone to check the time as the minutes flash by. You search your contact list for the agent's number but then decide to wait and see if you can find the building on your own. You grab a quick hot dog because you're famished from having skipped breakfast and don't know how long the meeting will go. But you hardly taste the meat and mustard because you're going over your proposal point by point in your head. If she does find a publisher to buy your book, how long will it take for the book to come out? Your thoughts are suddenly months in the future.

Or perhaps you're a forester working for a large timber company and you're cruising a section of the company's property marking trees for harvest. You estimate the potential board feet for each tree by measuring its girth and height with a digital tape measure equipped with a laser for better accuracy. Your boss is pressuring you to increase the yield, but the drought has allowed pests and disease to weaken the stand. The harvest plan will need to be adjusted downward, and that won't make anyone happy. Also you're pressed for time, you have a lot of ground to cover and you continually consult your hand-held GPS to see where you are. You come upon a stream and find a couple of guys fishing. The property is posted, signs everywhere. You smell smoke and see the smoldering remains of a fire and know that's not good either. Last thing the company needs now with these drought conditions is a fire. But you're not sure how to deal with the trespassers. You look closely at their waists to see if they are armed. You consider calling the police on your cell.

In these last two scenarios you activate the *logos* region of your brain so you can evaluate and act upon specific elements of your city and woodland experience.

A last way to appreciate the difference between *mythos* and *logos* knowing is to observe people at a party. We have a social convention that requires we use our *mythos* knowing when meeting a person for the first time. In other words, we take the person in all at once: the face, hair, clothes, smile, tone of voice, possibly the scent of aftershave or perfume. These impressions strike our senses at the same moment, as does the excited babble of the other voices around us, the splash of wine being poured into a glass, someone laughing at a joke. *Mythos* knowing is appropriate for such situations because it is friendlier, even though it can leave us vulnerable to being duped. An undercover police officer, however, uses his *logos* knowing almost exclusively when confronting a new social situation, as does a professional gambler or a con artist sizing up a mark. Could that scratch on the back of his hand be from the broken bedroom window? Ah, he tugs on his ear when he's bluffing. Her voice takes on an angry, resentful tone when she's talking about her rich aunt. That's what the cop, the gambler, and the con artist need to know.

* * *

Here's a chart comparing the characteristics of *mythos* and *logos* knowing. We've looked briefly at some of these differences and will explore others in the following chapters:

MYTHOS	*LOGOS*
sensory	symbolic
emotional	intellectual
holistic	reductionist
immediate	sequential
group-identity	individualistic
tribal	nationalistic
honor	expedience
gift-giving	commodity exchange
legend	historic fact

An interesting bit of history: in the nineteenth century the Chinese residents of San Francisco considered writing so sacred that they assigned certain individuals to walk around Chinatown and gather up any scrap of paper with writing on it they found on the ground. They then burned these scraps in a ceremonial clay pot to signify the honored place printed language held in traditional Chinese culture. This custom, however, was discontinued after the 1906 earthquake because it became impossible to collect all the printed paper that lay scattered about.

Another story I came across while researching the California gold rush also points to the difference between *mythos* and *logos*. As Americans headed west in their covered wagons in the 1850s, they reached a place in Nevada where the overland trail split in two, one trail going west and north toward the Oregon Territory and the other bending south and west to reach the gold fields of California. To distinguish the two trails, someone nailed a sign to a tree with an arrow and the word OREGON painted on it. Below was another crude sign without words but just an arrow and the painted image of a large gold nugget. Maybe that's why so many *logos* knowing individuals settled in the Pacific Northwest where their descendants built businesses like Amazon and Microsoft, while the image-makers pushed on to California where their descendants created Paramount and 20th Century Fox, Lucas Films and Pixar. It does make you wonder.

CHAPTER 3

Trouble on Lick Mountain

SOME YEARS AGO, THE ESTEEMED cultural anthropologist Marshall McLuhan coined the phrase "The Medium is the Message." Perhaps he borrowed its catchy rhythm from the repeating Ms of his own name, but what exactly did he mean? Consult a dictionary and you will find that the word "medium" has a number of definitions: it can refer to something in the middle, as in "the suspect was of medium height," or if you want to contact your late rich Uncle Mortimer to find out where he hid his will, you might engage the services of a medium. The linseed oil that a painter uses to mix her pigments and transfer them to the canvas is also called a medium, as is a nutrient system for the artificial cultivation of bacteria. But when it comes to storytelling, the word medium refers to a technology or combination of technologies that enables a person to communicate a story to others as well as the cultural context in which that story is communicated. A cathedral, for example, is a sophisticated storytelling medium in that it combines a number of unique technologies including vaulted ceilings, impressive statuary, stained glass, and a system of large bells, with a liturgical calendar that mandates the color of clerical vestments to be worn and which saint to honor on which day. There is also a prescribed order of worship: a time to kneel, to stand, to profess your faith, and to come forward to receive communion. All of this makes up the medium of the cathedral through which the message of religion is conveyed.

At first glance, the book as a storytelling medium appears quite simple. It is a collection of printed sheets of paper bound together with thread and glue. (Or perhaps a few megabytes of data on an electronic device with an LCD screen and USB port.) That is the technology of the book. But for people to use the book as a medium they must first go to school and learn to read. They must then wrestle time away from the beast of necessity—a task I find more difficult with each passing year—and create an island of quiet and solitude, even inside a crowded subway car.

A political debate is, likewise, its own special kind of storytelling medium that relies on microphones, podiums, lighting, and television cameras. But there are also rules governing how many minutes each candidate can speak, who gets to ask the questions, and whether the audience is allowed to applaud or not.

So back to McLuhan: the point he wanted to make was that the story, the *content*, is not nearly as important as the communication *medium* that is used when it comes to influencing how people think and act. Back in 1968, this was a radical idea. Then as now people, in particular academics and critics, love to decipher the hidden and not so hidden meanings they find in novels, movies, and rock songs. What is a painting or sculpture trying to say? What was the intention of the artist? What message were they trying to send? The questions were invariably qualitative: is *Madame Bovary* a more significant novel than *Pride and Prejudice*? Or today, is *Hardball* on MSNBC better or worse than *Fox and Friends* on FOX News?

It was the premise that the human experience could be understood by examining the stories we tell ourselves that McLuhan challenged. Although he was a *logos*-knowing academic, a trained deconstructionist, he believed that arguing over content while ignoring the medium was to miss the point. Or as he liked to say, "It's the slab of meat the burglar brings to distract the guard dog."

McLuhan held that beliefs and behaviors are shaped by the medium, not the content: thus "The Medium is the Message."

Put another way: the tendency of a particular medium to favor one way of knowing over the other is a matter of some importance.

A few years ago, I attended an old-time music festival in Clifftop, West Virginia. I was there to interview people for my radio series on family stories while doing a bit of fiddling on the side. A woman I met named Suzette Bradshaw shared a fascinating story with me about her grandmother, who grew up on Lick Mountain in western North Carolina. The story concerned something that happened in the late 1800s when Suzette's grandmother was a little girl. A group of women missionaries had come down from the North to start a school and church on Lick Mountain. There were only two large extended families living on the mountain at the time, and Suzette's family supported the missionaries' efforts, believing that, as Suzette put it, "Reading and writing was probably a good thing." The other family, however, was staunchly opposed to the school. For one thing, the Northern women were "outsiders" and the mountain folks were not sure they could be trusted.

"They thought the missionaries were making fun of the local people because they were illiterate and poor. My grandmother remembered them shipping down huge wooden barrels of clothes that they would gather up in the cities in the North for the children to go through and find clothes to wear. And this offended many of the community who were, I guess, a very proud lot."

Then one Sunday the tension over the school erupted into violence.

"The men folk started shooting, and probably in all actuality they weren't really shooting at each other, they were just shooting, you know, shooting trying to scare each other or whatever. But my grandmother was present and she was terrified of the gunfire, she was really scared of the whole situation, and so in the midst of her panic and all this gunfire going back and forth, she ran out into the trail, I would say road, but basically they were log shanty kind of things where folks were living. So she runs out into the trail and one of the guys sees her, she was only five or six, I'm not sure how old, and one of the guys sees her and runs out to grab her to bring her back into the house. And when he runs out, they shoot him dead! My grandmother never got over the fact that she felt responsible for another person's death. She was a very docile person, a very peace-loving person all her life, and she would tell that story and say, 'There's nothing worth dying over.' I think she never ever got over feeling that she was responsible for some person dying because of an action that she took, even though she was just a child."

The missionaries eventually gave up on Lick Mountain and moved their school over a couple of mountain ridges, where in time it became Pfeiffer College in Misenheimer, North Carolina.

This story illustrates the inherent tendency of *mythos* knowing and *logos* knowing to oppose each other. The opposition takes place both inside our minds and externally in society, which ultimately is only a projection of what's going on inside all of us.

We could characterize the family who fought against the new school as backcountry hicks who wasted their days swigging moonshine, picking their teeth with matchsticks, and who didn't give a fig what happened to their children. But that I believe would be a mistake. A more accurate picture is that of an isolated and proud people who worried that the new medium of reading and writing would take their children away from them. They feared that by learning to read and write the children of Lick Mountain would reject the old ways and relationships; they would move to the cities, allowing the life the elders lived and cherished to die out.

And these parents were right. With the beckoning of expanded possibilities, the best and the brightest often *did* leave, whether from the mist-covered mountains of North Carolina or the rock-strewn fields of Ireland.

This is another defining characteristic of *logos* knowing. It focuses on the individual, while *mythos* knowing is more concerned with the collective, the whole, the community. Reading and writing are essentially solitary endeavors, while corn husking parties, square dances, and barn raisings are *mythos* friendly activities.

We often hear media pundits use the term "culture war" when trying to explain the differences between Republicans and Democrats, liberals and conservatives, those who live near the coasts and those who dwell in the Heartland. I think most people would agree that there has been a marked increase in social and civic discord in recent years, the moderate middle giving way to extremists, but if this constitutes a war, then it is a war between our ways of knowing, our two forms of consciousness, and it is being played out in a series of confrontations between groups aligned with either *mythos* or *logos* knowing. These battles are taking place on the streets, in polling booths, within the film industry, in front of abortion clinics, inside nightclubs, on the National Mall, at school board meetings, and of course on the 24-hour cable news channels.

CHAPTER 4

A Day at the Cathedral

A REVOLUTION IS TAKING PLACE within the industrialized countries of the world today. It is a revolution of consciousness, the pendulum of political and cultural authority swinging away from *logos* knowing toward *mythos* knowing, and it is driven less by individuals than by new communication mediums. This sort of paradigm shift has occurred only a few times in recorded history. The prehistoric, preliterate world was by definition comprised of *mythos* knowing societies. Then writing was invented and a small administrative class came into being that included scribes who were skilled at making lists: so many amphorae of olive oil from Nineveh, so many blocks of salt from Cilicia, so many ingots of copper from Egypt. Scribes also set down on clay tablets and scrolls of papyrus revered myths such as *The Epic of Gilgamesh*, which until then had been transmitted orally. In some societies astronomers used the new technology of writing to record the positions of the stars and planets. But these societies remained primarily *mythos* oriented because the source of political power came from the *mythos*-laden rituals of kingship and religion.

Then the Greeks came along and the pendulum began to move in the direction of *logos* knowing. The Greeks popularized writing and reading, putting *logos* knowing in a position of greater influence over human affairs. Likewise, they made significant contributions in the fields of mathematics, engineering, metallurgy, animal husbandry, and botany that opened up the possibility for even more technological innovation. They developed schools of philosophy under the guidance of thinkers such as Socrates (470-399 BC) and his student Plato (428-348 BC) that sought to define and foster ethical social behavior. Laws were written down and the Greeks built libraries and schools and used written documents to regulate trade and govern their colonies.

Being a transition people, however, the Greeks still retained their institutions of *mythos* knowing; their temples, oracles, and elaborate rituals still held significant weight in their society. Rich and poor practiced magic and sorcery, drank potions to fall in love or call on the dead, and wore amulets to ward off the "evil eye," even though the new *logos* thinkers rejected these practices. Plato, for instance, aghast at such behaviors, demanded that those who practiced magic be punished.

This swing toward *logos* knowing continued during the military conquests of Alexander the Great. The son of a Macedonian king, Alexander was tutored from an early age by Aristotle who many consider the greatest *logos* thinker of the Classical period. Alexander incorporated many *logos* knowing techniques into his war-making and civil administration. He spread Greek culture, along with the Greek alphabet and textual literacy, into northern Africa and eastward into Asia and as far as the northern provinces of present-day India.

There is a well-known story that illustrates Alexander's talent for trumping *mythos* knowing with *logos* knowing. While wintering in Gordium in 334 BC, Alexander was presented with a challenge. There was a sacred cart in Gordium that was bound to its yoke with a knot that no one could untie. The residents of the city believed that whoever could untie the knot and separate the cart from the yoke would rule over all of Asia, a situation similar to the Arthurian legend of the sword in the stone. But whereas Arthur was pure *mythos*, a hero blessed by destiny and the training of a wizard to become king, Alexander was forced, in true *logos* fashion, to break the problem down into its component parts. The knot was made of a long strip of cornel bark and try as Alexander might, he could find neither its beginning nor end. Meanwhile, his generals and soldiers were watching, and Alexander knew that if he failed to untie the knot they would lose confidence in his ability to lead them in their upcoming invasion of Persia. They *had* to believe in him, in the myth of Alexander the Great, if he was to have any chance of success. (Ironically, he figured this out using his ability for *logos* knowing.)

So, according to one version of the story, he used a very sharp sword to cut the knot in such a way that it appeared as if he had untied it. In a more interesting and revealing version, he turned to the *logos* knowing part of his brain to discover that the knot was tied around a belaying pin that was jammed into the drawbar. Since it was the pin, not the knot, that was really holding the cart to the yoke, he was able to remove the pin, bypassing the knot altogether, thus tricking the people of Gordium into believing he had untied the knot. Whichever version of the story is true, the city was happy to proclaim him the future ruler of Asia.[4]

---

4. The expression "cutting the Gordian knot" is often used today to describe the act of breaking through a complicated and intricate problem that cannot be solved on its own terms. The future of Medicare, the Israel/Palestinian conflict, global warming, the Federal deficit have each been described as a Gordian knot looking for its Alexander, an indicative mix of *mythos* and *logos* imagery.

Here then is another difference between *mythos* and *logos* knowing: *mythos* knowing believes in destiny, in gods that ordain who succeeds and who doesn't, while *logos* knowing trusts in free will. Alexander believed he had the courage, skills, and determination to conquer Asia, and, if this coincided with destiny, then great; if not, he would do it anyway. He refused to regard himself as the plaything of the gods. He was an individual in charge of his own fate, a *logos*-becoming man.

Sadly, however, Alexander the Great also suffered from a serious mother complex, a bipolar disorder, and in the later part of his short life, a runaway addiction to alcohol—he died when he was thirty-two—and in the end reverted back to the *mythos* side of his personality, claiming he was the son of Zeus-Ammon. Suffice it to say, this did not go down well with his followers and the whole rule-the-world affair ended badly.

The Romans were the next team to come to bat in Europe. Compared to the Greeks and Alexander, the Pax Romana was *logos* knowing on steroids. Whereas the Greeks fashioned their buildings out of stone, the Romans built theirs using poured concrete. They also built a series of impressive aqueducts capable of carrying water from lakes and rivers to cities many miles away. They pioneered the use of crop rotation and built walled terraces so they could cultivate hillsides more productively. They also invented a wheeled plow that could turn heavy soil using a double-edged blade, a significant improvement over the wheeless ard with its single-edged blade that was limited to plowing shallow furrows in light soils.

But it is here we encounter an example of how a society based on one way of knowing can create a technology that inadvertently helps the other way of knowing come to power. The Romans were masters at road building, an activity requiring *logos* planning of the first order: avenues had to be cleared through dense forests, low-lying ground had to be drained, filled, and graded, and bridges needed to be designed and built to cross rivers. What the engineers and their superiors didn't foresee, however, was that these very roads would provide the barbarians living on the fringes of the Empire the ideal means to invade Rome. Because of these well-constructed thoroughfares, the enemy was able to march into the heart of the Empire and sack the capital city without being inconvenienced by forests, swamps, and rivers. The invasions were so swift, in fact, that the Roman military command simply did not have the time to adequately respond, and before they knew it, the barbarians were at the gates—not once, but repeatedly, thanks to the superb Roman highway system.[5]

The Romans also embraced the *logos* idea of interchangeable parts when equipping their armies. As letters are interchangeable, one P is the same as another P, an M is like other Ms, so too were the swords and shields borne by Roman legionaries. In weight, length, and materials, each sword and shield were identical to all the others. Interestingly, the standard Roman sword called a gladius was inferior to other swords of the period, but like the ubiquitous AK-47 of today, it proved to be a durable and effective weapon, especially when used in concert with the highly coordinated tactics of the Roman legion.

The Roman love of efficiency also worked against the Empire's interests when they began training and promoting

5. Maybe they could have slowed the Goths and Huns down if they'd installed some toll booths along the way. But alas, it would take more than 1,500 years for Mel Brooks to come up with that idea. And speaking of films, there is a great scene in the Monty Python film *The Life of Brian* where members of the People's Front of Judia compare Roman *logos* knowing with traditional *mythos* knowing that begins with the line: "They bled us white, the bastards. They've taken everything we had. And not just from us! From our fathers, and from our father's fathers" and ends with the line, "All right, but apart from the sanitation, the medicine, education, wine, public order, irrigation, roads, the fresh-water system, and public health, what have the Romans ever done for us?"

Germans, Gauls, and other leaders of conquered people to the highest ranks of the military command structure, believing these commanders would give their undivided allegiance to Rome and the *logos*-oriented rule of Pax Romana. Yet despite their *logos* training, the talented German and Gallic generals were *mythos* people at heart and remained fiercely loyal to their clans. So it followed that a number of these new generals led the invaders south along the Roman-built roads toward Rome, and the rest, as Gibbon would say, is history.

We don't normally think of roads as mediums of communication, but that's an important part of what they are. Just think where Paul Revere would have been without roads, or Wells Fargo, or FedEx. So with the Romans in mind, move forward in time and consider the terrorist attacks of September 11, 2001, only instead of physical roads we are dealing with electronic roads. The Internet came into existence through the joint efforts of two highly *logos* institutions: the military and the academy. The beliefs and behavior of the 9-11 attackers, by contrast, were essentially informed by *mythos*-knowing religious fundamentalism. They faced enormous logistical challenges, as daunting as any swamp or forest faced by the Huns. They had to find flights that would arrive at their targets within minutes of each other, denying the Air Force sufficient time to scramble fighter jets and shoot them down, while making sure each was a transcontinental flight so the aircraft would be fully loaded with fuel. What's more, the attackers and their superiors were based in different cities and needed a secure way of staying in touch with each other. They accomplished all this by using the Internet: airline web sites for detailed flight information and ticketing and postings in chat rooms for communications.

The weapons the terrorists used to carry out their attacks were as far apart in technical sophistication as imaginable: commercial jetliners that cost in the neighborhood of $70 million each and $4 box cutters fitted with disposable three-inch razor blades.[6]

The jet airplane was developed and deployed for military use by the Germans during World War II. In many ways, the jet airliner represents the highest achievement of *logos* knowing. For training, the 9-11 attackers attended commercial flight schools where they learned to pilot the jets using computer-generated flight simulators—another example of *logos*-based technology being used by *mythos*-knowing individuals to destroy the *logos* institutions that created them.[7]

Returning to our pendulum, *logos* knowing reached its extreme position around 170 AD during the reign of the Roman Emperor Marcus Aurelius. His book of personal notes to himself called *Meditations* has inspired *logos* thinkers down through the ages. In it he writes:

"The prime principle then in man's constitution is the social. And the second is not to yield to the persuasions of the body, for it is the peculiar office of the rational and intelligent motion to circumscribe itself, and never to be overpowered either by the motion of the senses or the appetites, for both are animal; but

6. Cost based on the Boeing 757, the model of jet that crashed into the Pentagon. As far as symbolism goes, the terrorists succeeded in striking the two building complexes most associated with *logos* knowing on the planet: one housing the leaders of the most technologically sophisticated military power the world has ever known, the other representing the capital-based global economic system.

7. Osama bin Laden, the founder of the jihadist organization al-Qaeda responsible for the 9-11 attacks, was the scion of a powerful and wealthy Saudi family that made its fortune in building and road construction. Raised a devout Wahhabi Muslim, bin Laden studied engineering and public administration at King Abdulaziz University in Jeddah, Saudi Arabia, before committing himself fully to his religion. Ironically, his father was killed in 1967 in an airplane crash when his American pilot misjudged a landing. His eldest stepbrother and head of the bin Laden family was killed in 1988 when he accidentally flew a plane into power lines in Texas.

the intelligent motion claims superiority and does not permit itself to be overpowered by the others. And with good reason, for it is formed by nature to use all of them. The third thing in the rational constitution is freedom from error and from deception. Let then the ruling principle holding fast to these things go straight on, and it has what is its own."

With the decline and fall of the Roman Empire in the West, however, the pendulum swung back toward *mythos* knowing, ushering in the Dark Ages and the dominance of the Roman Christian Church.[8]

Gone were the familiar *logos*-knowing institutions of Rome, the unified military command, public libraries, governmental administrative services, and the courts. In their place was Holy Mother Church. Among the clergy and church leaders, *logos* knowing continued to be valued and nurtured, which is understandable given that there were thousands of churches, cathedrals, monasteries, and convents to build and manage, theological questions to debate and rule upon, and large sums of money to be collected and invested, the very stuff of *logos* knowing. But in its mediation with the people and their rulers, the Church relied on *mythos* knowing techniques to make their influence felt. Their job, as they saw it, was to provide the faithful with stories and heightened sensory experiences to help

---

8. Given the constraints of this particular medium, the book, and the number of pages that can reasonably fit within its covers, we will confine our history of storytelling technologies/mediums to Europe and the United States beginning more or less with the Middle Ages. Another reason, to be honest, is that as an American of Irish and English ancestry who was raised as a Christian of the Roman Catholic variety, this is the history I'm most familiar with. A fascinating tale could be told about how these mediums played a major role in shaping the history of Asia, Africa, the Middle East, and the Americas before Columbus, and perhaps someone will take up that task in the future.

make life endurable, and perhaps even meaningful, despite the constant threat of disease, famine, and war. If we can separate the content from the medium, as McLuhan suggests, if we can put aside the complex religious doctrine of the Holy Roman Catholic Church (which included blood-ransom and an afterlife composed of heaven, hell, purgatory, and limbo) and train our attention instead on the various technologies the Church employed as it went about its business, we will begin to see why even kings had to bow before her.

One of the Church's most potent technologies for enhancing *mythos* knowing was the Gothic cathedral. Even with our jaundiced eye in this age of Trump Towers and "the Strip" in Las Vegas, Notre Dame in Paris still manages to steal our breath away. Imagine then the experience of a lowly serf passing through the giant ornate doors to enter a spacious forest of stone pillars, like mighty oaks, holding up an arched ceiling, so far above his head as to mimic the heavens. Radiant colors stream through tall stained glass windows to dazzle his eyes, a world apart from the scraped, dried animal hides that cover the windows of the cramped, smoke-choked huts of his village. Then a priest or the bishop appears in rustling vestments made of linen and velvet, perhaps even silk. How vivid the colors appear to him—violet, red, green, or gold depending on the season—compared with the his own humble attire of rough homespun cloth dyed with walnut hulls and other local plants. Every day our serf must endure the stench of animal dung and human waste, while here inside this magical building, his nose tingles with the sweet rarefied aroma of incense from faraway lands. There are the sounds also, the pealing of ponderous bells that call the faithful to worship, the trance-producing chanting of monks, the sonorous, angelic tones of an organ that rattle his loose teeth and tickle the little hairs inside his ears until they quiver with pleasure.

After the priest consecrates the Host, the serf might come forward, fall to his knees, and with eyes closed, hold out a tongue that knows only the taste of coarse barley bread to receive a communion wafer made from delicate and savory wheat flour.

And everywhere strange textures welcome his hand, the smooth polished wood of the benches, the cool marble of the communion rail.

No wonder after an hour or two of this, the serf is so blissed out, his *mythos* knowing channels tuned in and vibrating, that the priest can tell him just about anything, and he believes it without a second thought.

Thus, the Church employed her highly refined *mythos*-knowing technologies to spread her influence throughout Europe, raking in tithes, titles, and lavish gifts of land and châteaux.

Since the beginning of time, the warlords, those hairy-armed men of action clutching bloodstained swords, have been forced to negotiate deals with the mythmakers in their funny hats. It doesn't matter if the warlord is a Chaldean or Visigoth, a Celt or Aztec; without the willing obedience of the common people to fill his larder with meat and grain, his hearths with seasoned wood, his ranks with sturdy soldiers, and his bed with women, no warlord can continue for long being a warlord.

And since there are usually a half-dozen or more competing warlords in any one area at a given time along with the tendency of alpha males to vie with each other for supremacy, it is up to the mythmakers, those who own and operate the influence-producing storytelling mediums, to tell people precisely which warlord they should support.

Let's say you are a power-hungry thug who calls himself Duke Somebody or Other and your burning ambition is to become king, even though a bunch of competing ruffians called barons control different parts of the countryside. So you get together with the local bishop and come to "an understanding." The bishop promises to direct his priests to preach that you are really a great guy and that God desires that you be king. The bishop might even run out the old saw about the "divine right of kings," and, if any of the other barons gets his nose out of joint and decides to stir up trouble, the bishop will excommunicate the miscreant. The people will then naturally turn against the wayward baron because he's going to hell and they don't want to go with him. Game. Set. Match. You become king and the loser is sent packing.

In exchange for all this, you as the new king must promise to give the Church money, land, a place at court, and most importantly, a monopoly on mythmaking throughout the kingdom. Because it takes serious money and brainpower to build all those cathedrals, churches, and abbeys and how would you like it if some charismatic orator from out of town showed up one day and began preaching an alternate theology? Well, the bishop won't stand for any of that and he fully expects you to backstop the Church, even to the point of providing muscle for heretic burnings.

"Because fair is fair," says the bishop. "You get to wear the crown, but we put it on your head. So, what do you say? Do we have a deal?"

The warlord, in other words, has to purchase the *content*, the compelling story that justifies his rule, from the mythmakers who own and operate the dominant *mediums* of storytelling, and, in 12th century Europe, those mediums were churches, cathedrals, and monasteries.

Also, to be fair, there were many sincere and selfless men and women inside the Church who used their influence to alleviate suffering, limit the brutality visited upon the weak by the strong, and give people something enduring to believe in, to hope for. As the historians Will and Ariel Durant observed: "To the unhappy, the suffering, the bereaved, the old, it has brought supernatural comforts valued by millions of souls as more precious than any natural aid. It has helped parents and teachers to discipline the young. It has conferred meaning and dignity upon the lowliest existence, and through its sacraments has made for stability by transforming human covenants into solemn relationships with God."

In an important way too, the Church was a modernizing force in European history, especially during the later Middle Ages. It was the Roman Christian Church that organized and preserved much of society's *logos*-based knowledge and helped establish and enforce a rule of law among monarchs. Like Aristotle who taught the young Alexander, priests and monks helped foster *logos* knowing among the future rulers of Europe. But in terms of power relationships, the Church continued to function as the primary mythmaker that held the sacred, Reality-reflecting shield.

Then something happened around the 13th century in a monastery in Germany that nudged the *mythos-logos* pendulum in the opposite direction. The monks of the monastery, as part of their religious discipline, gathered in the chapel several times a day to pray. One of those times was called "matins," and in wintertime matins came before sunrise. This meant one of the brothers had to stay awake all night watching a notched candle so he would know when to get everyone else up for their prayers. Sometimes I suspect the poor man nodded off, which must have vexed the abbot no end, and there was the cost of the notched beeswax candles to consider.

So a bright *logos*-knowing monk came up with a mechanical device that sounded a chime at the appropriate time. He called it a "clock" from the Latin word "clocca," meaning bell, and he believed this invention would please God and further the work of the Church in the world.

Alas, it was not to be, because history, (one of the seven Greek muses), is fond of surprises. An inventor may believe he knows the best use for his new device, but then someone comes along who recognizes its true potential and transforms the world.

An example of this phenomenon closer to our time occurred when Gugliemo Marconi invented a radio transmitter so ships at sea could communicate with stations on shore. He thought of radio as a point-to-point communication technology. But it was Richard Sarnoff, a man who helped manage the radio office that handled the distress signals from the doomed Titanic, who realized that radio was in fact a "broadcast" technology. Sarnoff, who went on to run RCA and NBC, saw that radio was not a point-to-point medium, but a point-to-mass medium, the model for radio and television broadcasting from that day to this.

So it was for the clock in the 13th century, when the monastery's commercially minded neighbors came up with an alternative use for the new device. Rather than rely on the clock to wake them before sunrise so they could pray—they were not monks after all—they used it to make sure their workers all showed up at the same time, ate lunch at the same time, and went home at the same time—no bothersome Johnnies-come-lately throwing off the boss' schedule. They also started paying workers by the hour instead of by the day or the season.

Nor did the city fathers need the bells of the church to tell them the time, because they could build their own *logos* clocks. Business appointments could be made without needing to be near a church. Tanneries, iron works, and other manufacturing facilities could be built closer to the source of raw materials or waterpower as long as someone owned a clock.

Thus the years wore on, and a man named Johann Gutenberg invented a device that used movable type to make books quickly and cheaply. Before Gutenberg and others of his ilk, each book had to be tediously copied by hand, letter by letter, with a sharpened reed or quill dipped in ink, or printed using carved wood blocks, one for each page, making books so expensive that only wealthy individuals and the Church could afford to own them. Gutenberg called his invention a "printing press" and believed it would please God by promoting the interests of His Church. To underscore that point, the first book he printed using his new device was the Latin Bible.[9]

The printing press, however, even more than the clock, proved to be a true game-changer. Like a spring that gushes only sparingly at first but grows over time into mighty torrent, it was not long before the printing press was flooding the world with books—affordable books that most people could buy and, with a little effort, read.

And read them they did: nobles and nailsmiths, merchants and millers, clerks and candlemakers alike. Before the printing press, people looked to the Church for their stories, a repertoire limited pretty much to the gospels and the lives of the saints. But now they could curl up with a book by themselves, their eyes moving across the page from one letter to the next, from word to word. And as they did this, they rewired the circuitry of their brains. Also, given the abundance of cheap books, people were encouraged to start schools where children could be taught to read and write. Some inside the Church welcomed all this book reading for the masses as an improvement in the human condition. There were others, however, who rightly

9. The struggle to translate the Bible from Latin, the language of the clergy, into the language of the common people is an epic tale full of villains and heroes, a prime example of how the forces of *mythos* and *logos* contend with each other throughout the course of human history.

divined the threat textual literacy posed to the Church's political and cultural authority, and they sought to install valves to limit the flood. One was to burn books, sometimes with the author. Another was to require publishers of books that in any way touched on religious or spiritual matters to apply to the Church for an "imprimatur," an official seal that, when granted, must be printed on the front page of the book. The imprimatur assured the reader that the Church fathers judged the book free of heresy. No seal of approval? Put the book down or risk damning your immortal soul to everlasting hellfire.

The Catholic imprimatur was still in force during my youth. In fact, when my mother converted to Catholicism in 1941 while attending a Catholic college, she balked when a priest at the college explained that the Church forbade its members from reading certain books. She assured the priest that she was willing to go along with the rest of it—attending mass on Sundays and high holy days, eating fish on Fridays, and refraining from using artificial means of birth control, but she refused to allow the Church to dictate what she could or could not read. This tug-of-war with the priest lasted several months with the priest insisting the issue was nonnegotiable, that following rules was what being a Catholic was all about. But in the end, my mother wore him down and he told her that if the prohibition against reading banned books was the only impediment to her becoming a Catholic, then she should read any book she wanted but "just don't tell anybody."

My own experience with the Catholic Church was a strange and fascinating blend of *mythos* and *logos* knowing. From first through eighth grade I attended St. Therese's Elementary School in Paterson, New Jersey, which was run by female members of the Dominican order. The sisters wore traditional black and white habits with a cross on a chain about their necks and rosary beads dangling from their belts. Except for my fifth grade teacher, Sister Cornelia, they were a rather stern bunch, which perhaps was necessary given that each had to manage a class of between forty-five and fifty rambunctious students.

The nuns made us keep our desks in nice straight rows and taught us how to decipher straight lines of squiggly blotches of ink on paper. They taught us to write our own squiggly blotches in nice straight lines and, when I misbehaved, they accused me of being "out of line," with my penance being to write fifty to a hundred times on the blackboard in nice neat lines statements like, "I will not . . ."

So that is what we did in class; we trained the *logos* part of our young brains with lots of repetition. But once each day, the sisters instructed us to close our books and writing tablets and line up by the door. We would then march down the hallway with the other classes to the church, where we would dip the tips of our fingers into a brass wall container filled with holy water and make the sign of the cross while genuflecting and whispering the words, "In the name of the Father, the Son, and the Holy Ghost, Amen."

All about us were delicately carved and painted statues—prime examples of Old-World craftsmanship—of St. Therese, the Little Flower, our school's namesake, holding a bouquet of lilies, St. Joseph with his carpenter's square and the young boy Jesus standing by his side, the sad-eyed Mary, mother of God, and above the altar the life-sized corpse of Christ the Crucified, his head wreathed with thorns and blood trickling down his forehead, his hands and feet driven through with nails, and an open wound on his side where the Centurion thrust his spear.

For the complete story of the crucifixion in visual form, we could turn our attention to the Stations of the Cross, fourteen carved wall plaques that ran up one side of the church and down the other, each depicting a scene from that fateful day: Jesus being condemned to death by Pilate, Jesus falling under the weight of the cross, Jesus meeting his mother, Veronica using her veil to wipe the sweat and blood from Christ's face only to have the veil miraculously retain His image, and on through His crucifixion and burial.

School was no longer about squiggly blotches of ink on paper and cold straight lines nor were our teachers mere grammarians and mathematicians. Instead, they were storytellers full of tales about angels delivering divine messages to mortals, Satan tempting their Savior in the desert, water being turned into wine, lepers cured by the touch of a hand, and a multitude fed on only five loaves and two fish.

Then it was back to the classroom and the remainder of the day was devoted to abstract analytical thinking—a schizophrenic kind of education, but the best accommodation with the Age of Reason that Mother Church could manage at the mid-point of the 20th century. "You want rational thinking, no problem, we'll give you top-notch rational thinking. Only we'll allow time for that older sensual kind of knowing that extends beyond the bounds of the visible world, where all manner of mysteries and marvels abide."

Maybe that's why I became an altar boy. It was like watching a movie and being in it at the same time. I would kneel and ring the little bell as the priest genuflected and then raised the host above his head, the swish of his moiréd purple vestments filling my young ears. I would bring him a small glass pitcher of water and a towel so he could wash his hands. The priest would call out in Latin and I would answer in the same strange tongue as we faced the altar, our backs to the congregation. But I could sense them there in the pews: the solitary old women dressed in black thumbing their rosary beads, the little kids squirming and poking each other, the somber veterans of the Second World War passing the baskets for the collection.

It would be many years until I began to appreciate how similar these two experiences were: celebrating mass and watching a movie.

CHAPTER 5

The New Liturgy

WITH THE COMING OF THE RENAISSANCE, the pendulum of consciousness began to swing away from *mythos* knowing in the direction of *logos* knowing, rending the fabric of European society. Like Gutenberg, Galileo was thinking about God when he built his first telescope in 1609, wanting people to more fully appreciate the majesty of the heavens God had created. But Galileo lived in what was still a predominately sensory WYSIWYG—what-you-see-is-what-you-get—age. So if the senses tell you the world is flat and the sun orbits the earth, then that's how it must be.

But Galileo's device proved that the unaided senses can lie, an accusation which extended as well to the institution that drew its raison d'être from *mythos* knowing, the Church. The upshot was that the Church condemned Galileo as a heretic and put him under house arrest, which psychologically crushed the poor man. Nor would they allow his remains to be buried in consecrated ground after his death

Thus brilliant people invented exciting new technologies believing they were pleasing God and His servants on earth when, in fact, these technologies were better suited to a *logos-*

knowing world and would over time weaken the political and economic authority of the Church.

As with the barbarian invasions of Rome and the conflict on Lick Mountain, transitional periods are often marred by violence and social upheaval. People feel compelled to take sides. So it was with the Reformation. In Germany, Martin Luther, a priest and professor of theology, challenged the authority of the Church, not by preaching in the streets but by nailing a printed document to the door of All Saints Church in the university city of Wittenberg. His intention was to dispute point-by-point the Church's practice of selling indulgences, which were like "get out of jail free" cards in the game Monopoly that anxious sinners purchased with the assurance that their term of suffering in purgatory would be shortened. Within months, thanks to the printing press, the 95 Theses, as Luther's document became known, had gone viral reaching people all over Europe.

In 1560, the reformer John Knox set about transforming St. Giles Cathedral in Edinburgh, Scotland, by smashing all the statues and stained-glass windows and whitewashing the walls. Music was likewise banned in many of the new Protestant churches, as was incense, those perniciously sensual triggers. The altar was pushed to the back, if not removed altogether, and the pulpit brought forward upon which rested one of the new printed Bibles and from which the sacred texts, no longer in Latin but in the common vernacular, were read chapter and verse. In this way, the printed word became the heart of the liturgy.

The problem with the Reformation, however, was that by attacking the power of the Church, it also challenged the authority and legitimacy of the top warlords and the time honored rituals of kingship, forcing them to wage war in hopes of preserving a world that played by their rules. These conflicts were not viewed by those who participated in them as mere squabbles over territory or plunder, but over the fate of men's souls, and as such they were fought with a tenacity and brutality seldom matched in human history.

By the early part of the seventeenth century, however, the institutions of *logos* knowing were triumphing and we entered the Age of Reason. Industrialization followed close on the heels of textual literacy because both are manifestations of the same *logos*-knowing behavior: instead of stringing printed letters together on the page to make words, sentences, and paragraphs, you combine bolts, nuts, and gears along an assembly line to make engines, transmissions, and complete automobiles. Among the first countries to break free of the Church and embrace *logos* knowing as the preferred way of perceiving the world and making important decisions were England and Germany, and they led the way in industrialization.

Not only did the form of divine worship change radically with the ascendency of *logos* knowing, many of the ancient folk rituals like Harvest Home and May Day were abandoned or trivialized. The cottage loom gave way to the woolen mill; the farmer and farm laborer became the city dweller and factory worker. In Ireland, military forces under Oliver Cromwell strove to stamp out the Gaelic language and any vestige of the old customs. Throughout Europe, *logos*-knowing institutions, national legislative bodies and municipal governments, industrial and commodity-trading corporations, a professionalized military, and universities were heralded as the way of the future.

Thus the years passed and *logos* knowing ruled until a variety of new inventions sprang into existence from the very heart of *logos* knowing, from its ingenuity, organizational efficiency, and industrial capacity. And once more the pendulum reversed direction.

CHAPTER 6

Heigh Ho, Heigh Ho, It's Off to Work We Go

ONE OF THE EARLIEST *MYTHOS*-KNOWING communication mediums to come out of the Age of Reason and its attendant Industrial Revolution was photography. It was one thing to read about the horrors of the American Civil War, but to look at Matthew Brady's albumen-developed images of dead soldiers and horses scattered across the killing fields of Antietam, their bodies dismembered and bloated, was to "feel" the reality of war. In 1890, when people opened the book *How the Other Half Lives* and looked at Jacob Riis' photographs chronicling the appalling conditions many immigrants were forced to endure living and working in the tenements of New York City, they became troubled and wanted to do something to help. The same held true for the photographs taken by Lewis Hine of children working in cotton mills, glass factories, and coal mines. More often than not it was the visual experience of these bleak realities as opposed to the purely textual that spurred people to action.

Mark Twain, often described as the most popular man in America in his later years, fully appreciated the power of this new medium. In 1905 he wrote a scathing indictment of King

Leopold II of Belgium for pursuing a policy of torture and murder in the Congo that he titled *King Leopold's Soliloquy*. Pretending the king had written the document, Twain included this passage:

"The Kodak has been a sore calamity to us. The most powerful enemy that has confronted us, indeed. In the early years we had no trouble in getting the press to "expose" the tales of the mutilations as slanders, lies, inventions of busy-body American missionaries and exasperated foreigners who found the "open door" of the Berlin-Congo charter closed against them when they innocently went out there to trade; and by the press's help we got the Christian nations everywhere to turn an irritated and unbelieving ear to those tales and say hard things about the tellers of them. Yes, all things went harmoniously and pleasantly in those good days, and I was looked up to as the benefactor of a downtrodden and friendless people. Then all of a sudden came the crash! That is to say, the incorruptible *Kodak*—and all the harmony went to hell! The only witness I have encountered in my long experience that I couldn't bribe. Every Yankee missionary and every interrupted trader sent home and got one; and now—oh, well, the pictures get sneaked around everywhere, in spite of all we can do to ferret them out and suppress them. Ten thousand pulpits and ten thousand presses are saying the good word for me all the time and placidly and convincingly denying the mutilations. Then that trivial little Kodak, that a child can carry in its pocket, gets up, uttering never a word, and knocks them dumb!"

By the midpoint of the nineteenth century, Thomas Edison, along with a few others, discovered how to record and play back sound. Beginning with cylinders made of paraffin and beeswax and moving on to round flat platters fashioned from celluloid, the early phonographs brought a new world of music into the homes of farmers and factory workers, merchants and miners.

A few years ago my wife and I were asked to perform at a St. Patrick's Day banquet. I had recently acquired a wind-up phonograph in an upright wooden case, the kind where you control the volume by how far you open the two small doors on the front. After playing a selection of traditional Irish fiddle tunes, I concluded the concert with a story about a young woman who emigrated from Ireland to the United States at the turn of the twentieth century. She came from a musical family in Sligo, someone was always stopping by the house to play the fiddle or penny whistle or sing a ballad, and so she grew up loving music. In time she married a young Irishman who took her to western Pennsylvania where he found work as a coal miner. It was a rough life and she heard very little music in the coal camp, which was a great sorrow to her. Then on the evening of her twenty-eighth birthday a wagon pulled up in front of her house, and two men carried a large wooden crate inside where they pried it open with crowbars. And what was inside? At this point in the presentation I pulled a cover off my own phonograph, which had stood unnoticed throughout our performance on the right side of the stage. "It was a machine for playing music," I said. "It was a birthday present from her husband and it came with a dozen records by the great Irish tenor John McCormack. Imagine how she must have felt as that sweet enchanting music filled the silent corners of her modest coal company house for the first time, the memories it brought back of her childhood among the green hills of her native Ireland."

I placed a record on the turntable and wound the phonograph using the crank that stuck out the side. There were several hundred people in the banquet hall, most of them Irish-American, who only moments earlier had been eating, drinking, laughing, and talking. But when I placed the needle on the old vinyl 78, the room became utterly quiet and remained so for the next four minutes as John McCormack sang "The Rose of Tralee."

Afterwards, people came up to us with tears in their eyes. They said they felt as if they had been transported back in time to the world of their ancestors. This is the power of *mythos* knowing, and the phonograph was just one of the new technologies reshaping the character and behavior of the American people.[10]

My mother, born in 1924, came of age when radio was king. She thrilled to the adventures of *Jack Armstrong, the All American Boy*, and Lamont Cranston, "a wealthy young man about town," who in reality was none other than *The Shadow*, an avenger with the ability to cloud men's minds with hypnotism so they couldn't see him. Like so many other Americans, she also laughed at the antics of *Fibber McGee and Molly* and *Amos 'n Andy*.

On a Sunday evening in 1938 when she was fourteen, she was out with her best friend Gladys when they happened to turn on the radio and heard that Martians with death rays had invaded Grover's Mills, New Jersey, only an hour from where they lived. Frightened out of their wits, they tried for more than an hour to reach their parents at home on the telephone to warn them. But alas, they never got through because the switchboards were jammed by thousands of other terrified listeners trying to reach their loved ones.[11]

10. My friend Utah Phillips pointed out after the concert that the material science necessary to make the original phonograph actually existed as far back as the Renaissance. The only thing lacking was the idea to assemble the elements together in that way. Had someone figured this out, we might have audio recordings of interviews with Leonardo DiVinci and Michelangelo or actors performing in plays written and directed by Molière and Shakespeare.

11. Based on a novel by H. G. Wells, *War of the Worlds* was performed by the Mercury Theater of the Air, a company of radio actors founded by Orson Wells and John Houseman. In an effort to create an aura of realism, the first two thirds of the program was presented as a series of simulated "news bul-

As a young woman, my mother danced to broadcasts of the Jimmy Dorsey and Glenn Miller bands and, when the Depression hit, she listened with rapt attention to the reassuring voice of Franklin Roosevelt giving his "fireside chats."

During the war years, she watched Movietone newsreels and listened to Edward R. Murrow broadcasting from the rooftops of London as shells from antiaircraft batteries exploded the black sky above him. The experience of live radio and television coverage is now commonplace, but in my mother's day it was a novel experience to *feel* you were part of a war as it happened despite being thousands of miles away. Bill Shirer, Morrow's radio colleague during the war, described it well in his book, *The Nightmare Years, 1930-1940*:

"Instantaneous transmission of news from the reporter to the listener, in his living room, of the event itself, so that the listener could follow it just as it happened . . . was utterly new. There was no time lag, no editing or rewriting as in a newspaper. A listener got straight from a reporter, and instantly, what was taking place. The sound of a riot in Paris, of the Pope bestowing an Easter blessing in Rome, or of Hitler and Mussolini haranguing their storm troopers might tell you more than all the written descriptions a newspaper reporter could devise."

---

letins" that interrupted what pretended to be an ordinary program of musical entertainment. Slowly but surely the news bulletins became more ominous and alarming with one "on-the-scene" reporter describing the landing of a rocket machine in central New Jersey. Then the reporter's voice was cut off in mid-sentence as a heat ray emanating from the spacecraft began incinerating the crowd of onlookers. This rather innocent attempt to blend fiction with fact created a furor in the days following the broadcast with many newspapers and politicians castigating the Mercury Players for causing a panic. The stunt, how-ever, turned Orson Wells into an overnight national celebrity. He subsequently took his talents to Hollywood where he directed and acted in the film *Citizen Kane* based on the life of media mogul William Randolph Hearst. This more sophisticated mixture of fact and fiction is considered by many critics to be one of the finest films of all time.

I have spent a number of years working in radio myself. Sometimes when I transcribe an interview I am struck by how much smaller the text file is compared to the audio file. A three-minute-twenty-second interview recorded in mono, for instance, contains roughly 17,408 kilobytes of information (17 megabytes), while the same interview typed into a Microsoft Word document, including notes for pauses, laughter, a cough, contains just 32 kilobytes of information. So where did the remaining 17,376 kilobytes of data go? Well, there is the sound of a car driving by, the creak of the speaker's chair when he moves—even the sound he makes when moistening his lips before speaking. But for the listener the most compelling information might come from the tone and inflection the speaker uses when he says the word "dad," or the name of his hometown, the emotion embedded in the sound. All this is lost in the printed medium. No wonder people loved the new technology of radio, even if it meant allowing the fear and anxiety of war to penetrate the safety of their homes.

In many ways, World War II was a by-product of the emerging political and cultural power of *mythos* knowing. In Nazi Germany, Dr. Joseph Goebbels understood better than anyone how the new mediums of radio and film could be harnessed to influence human behavior, and, in Hitler, he had the perfect media demagogue, a man ready-made for the camera, microphone, and loudspeaker.

A little-known fact about Hitler is that his first speech, given in October 1919 in the basement of a beer hall, turned into a disaster as he lost control of the rowdy crowd and was nearly driven from the hall. So he took lessons in oratory and performance techniques from a man named Hermann Steinschneider, a professional magician and clairvoyant who adopted the stage name Erik Jan Hanussen to conceal the fact that he was Jewish. It was this training that enabled Hitler to hold huge crowds spellbound using only his voice and gestures. In fact, the first time Goebbels went to hear Hitler speak, he wrote in his diary, "I have heard the Messiah."

Goebbels was one of those transitional individuals who appear at a crossover point in history where one way of knowing gives way to the other. As a young man during the First World War, he tried to serve in the army but was turned away because of a deformed foot and leg. He therefore turned to the world of books and became a voracious reader. He eventually earned his doctorate in literary history from Heidelberg University, and, when his father acquired a radio set in 1923, he scoffed in his diary, "The modern mind-narrowing device. Everything piped in! The philistine's ideal!"

Yet despite being a skilled *logos*-knowing organizer, Goebbels possessed a gift for oratory, which led him to embrace radio and film and transform them into effective avenues for delivering mythically charged propaganda.

"It hardly matters what we believe in, so long as we believe in something," proclaims a character in a novel Goebbels wrote, revealing the author's appreciation for the function and potential of the mythmaking mirror, the polished shield of Perseus. In fact, he practiced each pose and gesture in front of a mirror before giving a speech, understanding the powerful effect visual presentation had on an audience. This included the ceremonial use of flags and standards, the parading of massed brass bands, the carefully planned delayed arrival, and traveling around in large fancy automobiles.

As for this last need, the Daimler-Benz Company generously loaned or donated the use of their latest models to the top officials of the small but emerging Nazi Party. As a Daimler-Benz manager bragged in a memo in the company's archives, "We helped motorize the movement."

So here you have a petroleum-fueled transportation device made of steel, rubber, and leather, designed by top-notch *logos*-trained engineers, and built in a factory, transformed into a *mythos* medium with a significant persuasive impact. Hitler standing and saluting from the back of his Mercedes as it moves slowly through an adoring crowd conjures up the image of a king in his regal carriage or the god Apollo atop his golden chariot, the three-pointed Mercedes emblem and Nazi swastika, according to the archives, blending into each other in the eyes and imagination of the "German volk."

As early as 1931, Daimler-Benz was taking out large ads in a Nazi newspaper known for its virulent propaganda and anti-Jewish tirades. Hitler even held a portfolio of Daimler-Benz stocks that a company director administered for him. The same director also picked up the soon-to-be Führer at the gates of Landsberg Prison after Hitler finished his nine-month sentence for attempting to overthrow the elected government by force.

A decidedly more positive example of a transportation technology being used to foster *mythos* knowing involved the folk singer Pete Seeger, who, in the 1960s, was deeply distressed by the polluted condition of the Hudson River near where he lived. Being a accomplished storyteller and social justice activist, Seeger knew it takes more than credible information to change how people think and act. For a message to be effective, it must appeal to both the *logos-* and *mythos*-knowing parts of the brain, and one means of doing this is to marry a powerful mythic symbol with an enchanting ritual. As Emerson wrote: "A good symbol is the best argument and is a missionary to persuade thousands."

So Seeger joined forces with a committed cadre of environmentalists to build a sailboat like the ones that were in common use on the river in the early days of the Republic. They called their vessel the Sloop Clearwater and began sailing it up and down the river, stopping at towns along the shore and putting on festivals featuring folk music, storytelling, and ideas for cleaning up the Hudson. It is one of the most successful environmental public relations campaigns in American history and played a major role in raising awareness of the long-term effects of ecological destruction and what could be done to turn things around. The Sloop Clearwater still sails the Hudson River and continues to educate and entertain. It is a truly creative union of *logos* and *mythos* knowing.

Jump forward thirty years or so and we find the origin of another relationship between an automobile manufacturer and an emerging political leader. In 1990, the actor Arnold Schwarzenegger was in Oregon working on the film set of *Kindergarten Cop* when he noticed a convoy of Humvees roll past on their way to a nearby military base. It was love at first sight. Later, as reported in the *Washington Post*, the actor got to check out a Humvee up close where he marveled, "Look at those deltoids; look at those calves."

It wasn't long until Schwarzenegger had one of his own, converted by the manufacturer, AM General, so it could be driven legally on the streets of Los Angeles. Schwarzenegger then convinced AM General to produce a civilian line of Humvee-like vehicles, which they called the Hummer.

General Motors bought the Hummer line in 1999 and Schwarzenegger became the unofficial spokesman for the massive, fuel-hungry vehicles. He had already set his cap on becoming the next governor of California, but he had serious work to do if he hoped to win over minority and women voters. So he talked General Motors into funding a series of after-school programs in distressed inner-city neighborhoods to broaden his popularity. Following the 2003 special election that made Arnold Schwarzenegger the 38th governor of California, Hummer sales accelerated from approximately 20,000 units in 2002 to more than 71,000 units in 2006. By the end of his first term, however, due to rising oil prices and the threat of global warming, Schwarzenegger was forced to go "green," selling some of his own Hummers and converting three of the remaining four to run on biodiesel, vegetable oil, and hydrogen respectively. In February of 2010, having fallen on hard times in the aftermath of the global economic meltdown, General Motors pulled the plug on the Hummer line.

Again we see that the luxury automobile with its large wheels and abundance of shiny chrome can be a *medium* of *mythos* knowing employed by political operatives to convince the masses that the person inside the car is a leader worthy of their adoration and support. The Hummer was only one element in a *mythos*-knowing phenomenon that resulted in an action movie star with no previous legislative or administrative governmental experience being elected to run a state with a population of thirty-five million people and boasts the eighth largest economy on the planet.[12]

Returning to Goebbels and his genius for using *logos*-engineered and manufactured tools to serve Nazi-inspired *mythos* knowing ends, it is instructive to note that that many of the leading manufacturers of visual and audio technology in the world at that time were German, companies like Braun, Telefunken, Siemens, Beyerdynamic, Leica, and Agfa. One company, founded by the gifted audio engineer Georg Neumann, developed a condenser microphone in the early 1920s that was far superior to any other microphone available at the time. A

---

12. In recent years General Motors has gone to great lengths to market its Cadillac Escalade sports utility vehicle to rappers, professional athletes, and hip-hop wannabes. The company has held highly secretive, invitation-only events including one in the parking lot of a closed movie theater in Los Angeles to solicit suggestions from owners like rapper Snoop Dog and LA Lakers star Shaquille O'Neal on wheel designs, audio systems, and interior features.

large canister with a head like a golf ball, the model CMV3 gave the human voice its full dynamic range while sounding clearer, closer, and more authoritative. Not only did this revolutionary microphone communicate the words of the message, it also succeeded in conveying the emotion of the message and was used so often by Hitler, Goebbels, and other Nazis orators that it became known as the "Hitler flasche" (Hitler bottle) because its shape was reminiscent of a milk bottle.[13]

No one made better use of film as a medium of propaganda than the director Leni Riefenstahl who began her career as a film actress in Germany. In 1934, Hitler commissioned her to film the Nazi Party Congress that was held each year in Nuremberg. These ritualized mass gatherings were expertly choreographed by Albert Speer, Hitler's architect of the Third Reich, and included days and nights of marches, speeches, and bonfires. It was a psychologically transforming experience for the hundred thousand party members who attended each Congress. Using multiple camera crews, special film stock, and a variety of innovative filmmaking and editing techniques, she transformed what might have been a simple documentary into an extraordinary work of art, one in which her sponsor was elevated to god-like status. *Triumph of the Will* was shown in movie houses throughout Germany and in many other European countries, adding greatly to Hitler's popularity. It even won the coveted Gold Medal for cinema in France. [14]

13. Neumann microphones continued to set the standard for microphones following the war and were used to record artists such as Frank Sinatra, Ella Fitzgerald, Tony Bennett, and Bing Crosby. The Beatles used the Neumann U47 on nearly every track they recorded from 1964 to 1970, and today vintage Neumann microphones are so coveted by audio engineers that a single unit can fetch as much as $20,000.

14. *Triumph of the Will* was widely banned in the United States being considered little more than Nazi propaganda. A copy was kept at the Museum of

Although the film includes short segments of speeches by Hitler, Hess, and other Nazi leaders, it is the images that do the real work: the huge swastikas held aloft by eagles, the massed torchlight parades, the close-ups of individual party members calling out the names of their hometowns, and the Führer smiling, the Führer scolding, the Führer triumphant—the camera mounted on a special circular dolly on the stage shooting upward against a cloud-swept sky, the leader's strong chin in relief, the commanding glint of his unflinching eyes gazing out over the worshipful crowd—a prime example of the medium being the message.

"It had to be filmed the way an artist, not a politician, sees it," Ms. Riefenstahl said in 1993 when interviewed for a documentary about her life. "Hitler didn't want a political film. He wanted an artistic film. That's what he got."

When discussing her technique she said, "It's a feeling for the links between images, a connection between one picture and the next, or from one visual color range—say from gray tones—to another. It's like a musical composition: it's very important to put a climax at the right point in a film so that there is a continuous buildup. I tried a hundred different ways at the editing stage. It took me over five months. First I was working twelve hours a day, then fourteen, eighteen, and in the end twenty. That meant I couldn't do anything but sit at my editing suite trying to find ways to avoid jumps so it would all flow in an interesting way."

When Hitler came to power in 1933, the thirty-five-year-old Joseph Goebbels was given the job of Reich Minister of Propaganda and Public Enlightenment, a title Goebbels considered too cumbersome but one that Hitler liked. The position gave Goebbels direct control over radio, film, theater, and the press throughout Germany. From his personal diaries

---

Modern Art in New York City and was only shown to a select few.

we have a portrait of a man obsessed with film. He watched everything. His favorite American films were *Gone with the Wind* and Disney's *Snow White and the Seven Dwarves*. The kind of films the minister of propaganda despised were overtly political films such as the 1933 film *Hitler Junge Quex* (Hitler Youth Quest), in which the hero, a young boy, dies for the Führer. Goebbels preferred entertaining films because they kept people distracted from their political and financial problems. According to Fritz Hippler, a director who worked in Germany during the Nazi era, Goebbels held that film was the highest form of communication because it worked on the subconscious.[15]

Without the microphone, loudspeaker, radio transmitter, sound truck, movie camera, and phonograph, the Nazis may never have gained power. In keeping with this swing toward *mythos* knowing, Goebbels began to see that it was essential to attack the primary medium of *logos* knowing: the book. In April of 1933, Nazi-run student organizations at the nation's leading universities came up with the idea to stage mass book-burning rallies throughout Germany. They wanted to purge the literary culture of everything they deemed decadent and un-German, and they wanted Goebbels to provide both financial support and serve as the featured speaker at the rally that would be held in Berlin. For several weeks, the minister dithered; his own intellect had been enriched by many of the books listed for destruction. But in the end, he embraced the idea. In a square between the opera house and the university, the organizers erected a crisscross log pyre, while five thousand students began a torchlight march from several blocks away, ending at the square where trucks loaded down with books

15. Hitler was also crazy about movies and watched one nearly every evening. On the rare occasions when he couldn't, Hitler required his adjutant, Julius Schaub, to watch the film and relate the plot to him scene by scene the next morning. Perhaps it is a curious coincidence that the name of the town west of Berlin where films were made under the Nazis was called Babelsberg.

awaited them. Forty thousand Berliners packed the square and cheered as each author's name and offenses were read over loudspeakers, followed by their books being tossed into the ravenous bonfire.

As one witness observed, "I thought they'd all gone stark raving mad, particularly the womenfolk."

In every university town in Germany, books were consigned to the flames: on the Königsplatz in Munich, the Römerberg in Frankfurt, and the Castle Square in Breslau. In all upwards of 20,000 books were destroyed that night including the works of Thomas Mann, Jack London, Helen Keller, Upton Sinclair, Albert Einstein, and many others.

"These flames do not only illuminate the final end of the old era, they also light up the new," Goebbels told the world over the radio after mounting the swastika-festooned stage at midnight, his sharp features illuminated by the light of the huge bonfire, the air heavy with the tang of burning paper. "Never before have the young men had so good a right to clean up the debris of the past . . . The old goes up in flames, the new shall be fashioned from the flame in our hearts."

As with the Nuremberg rallies, Goebbels knew that for maximum effect, (always the little Doctor's watchword when it came to propaganda), those not physically present at the bonfires should experience the event vicariously. To this end he made sure the book-burnings were filmed and distributed throughout the Reich as movie newsreels.

The Nazis weren't the first people to burn books. Books by Islamic scholars, by Christian heretics, by "filthy-minded perverts" like James Joyce, whose novel *Ulysses* was burned in Boston, had all been targets. But the Nazis' approach to book burning in order of magnitude far surpassed anything that had come before. And even though they struck the same pose as earlier book burners, claiming the books were filthy and anti-

German and would corrupt the youth, their true motivation was a deep-seated anti-intellectualism, a fervent rejection of *logos* knowing, expressing itself in a concerted effort to tear down the book from its perch of cultural authority within German society. It was time, Goebbels and the students were telling their fellow citizens through both words and deeds, to *feel* the political realities of the day, savor the pulse of hot Aryan blood in their veins, swell their chests with national pride, and weep like children with love for the Führer. They should refuse to waste their time in stuffy classrooms, musty study halls, and dreary libraries merely reading about politics, all that sitting softened the muscles and made the heart grow cold and indifferent. Besides, reading, reflecting, and judging took too much time. *Mythos* knowing burns brightest in the present moment. If you must consider the past, then consider the mythic past when the great Aryan heroes first walked the earth. From those deep memories comes power and freedom from doubt.

So it was that Goebbels and Hitler had their way and the German people marched obediently off to destruction. Today the film *Triumph of the Will* is kept under lock and key by the German government out of a profound sense of shame.

And while we may rightly despise Goebbels, called by one of his biographers, "the hater of mankind," for all that he did, he did provide us with an object lesson in what happens when highly talented *logos*-knowing individuals seeking political, economic, or cultural power use *mythos*-knowing mediums to influence, dupe, divide, scare, flatter, and mislead the people with scant regard for the long-term consequences. It happened in the 1930s in Germany and there is little reason to believe it could not happen again.

CHAPTER 7

Every Man a King

BESIDES GERMANY, *MYTHOS*-KNOWING mediums transformed a number of other mid-twentieth century societies. As a young man, Joseph Stalin trained for the priesthood in his native Georgia but left the seminary to take both the *mythos* and *logos* knowing of that training into the rough and tumble arena of Russian politics. Once in power, he set about creating and refining what has become known as "the cult of the personality." Instead of venerating Jesus or St. Catherine, the Russian people were instructed to give their full devotion to Papa Joe, the all wise, courageous, and ever-vigilant. As the first General Secretary of the Communist Party of the Soviet Union's Central Committee, he ordered that the icons of orthodox Christianity be replaced with placards of the Leader and that the statues of the saints and patriarchs be exchanged with ones of himself. He also renamed cities and towns, many formerly honoring Christian saints, with variations on the name "Stalin."

Few men ever had a love affair with cinema to rival Joseph Stalin's. He built his own private movie theater inside the Kremlin where he, like Hitler, watched films almost every night, no matter what was happening in the outside world, even when the German Army was invading and destroying his country. *The Inner Circle*, a fascinating film made in 1991, is based on the real-life story of Ivan Sanshin who was Stalin's personal projectionist from 1939 until the dictator's death in 1953. The film charts the course of Shanshin's slow but steady corruption, his *logos*-knowing faculties blinded by a *mythos*-inspired hero worship as old as time itself. As part of Stalin's efforts to replace the mythmaking apparatus of the Orthodox Church with his own brand of Communism, he launched an ambitious project to build movie theaters in towns big and small throughout the Soviet Union. An impoverished cluster of houses far out on the steppe or in a hidden valley high in the Ural Mountains, places little touched by the Industrial Revolution, might fervently desire a modern sewer or public transportation system, a tractor factory or new school, but what they got instead was a movie theater showing films produced in government-owned or supervised studios, most extolling the virtues of the great leader, Stalin.

Even historical dramas played their part in advancing Stalin's political agenda. The Russian director Sergei Eisenstein directed a film in 1938 called *Alexander Nevsky* about the heroic efforts of the city folk of Novgorod to defeat an invading army of Teutonic knights in the 13th century. In the film, the knights conquer Pskov, where they massacre the inhabitants, but then Prince Alexander and the people of Novgorod retaliate, defeating the Teutonic invaders in a decisive battle on the frozen ice of Lake Chudskoe. *Alexander Nevsky* was Eisenstein's first dramatic film to use both sound and a stirring score by the composer Sergei Prokofiev.

Tensions between Nazi Germany and the Soviet Union were nearing a breaking point in 1938 when the film came out. It was unabashedly anti-German, anti-clerical, and anti-Catholic—

even the mitre of the knights' bishop was adorned with swastikas. Two weeks after the film's highly successful opening, however, Stalin signed the controversial Molotov-Ribbentrop Pact, a nonaggression treaty with Nazi Germany, and ordered the film pulled from distribution and locked away in a government vault. There it sat until June 22, 1941, when Germany, without warning, attacked the Soviet Union, prompting Stalin to rush the film out again to Soviet and western movie theaters, where it became a potent and mythic rallying cry for the Russian people. The film's message resonated with a rising tide of Russian nationalism: "We've defeated the hated Hun before and we can do it again."

Here in the United States, Franklin Roosevelt's "fireside chats" were broadcast over the airwaves from coast to coast and proved enormously effective in calming people's fears at a time when American banks were failing daily and families were losing their entire life savings. FDR also took advantage of the mythic potency of grand automobiles. The image of Roosevelt sitting behind the steering wheel of an open-top touring car flashing his famous Roosevelt grin, a cigarette holder clamped between his teeth, appealed greatly to his supporters. Here, they believed, was a man born to the manor but endowed with the common touch, a leader for all the people.

In fact, Franklin's mythic projection rivaled those of Hitler and Stalin, to such an extent that many people kept large framed photographs of him in their homes. A woman I interviewed for my radio program on family stories told me how her mother once got so mad at something Roosevelt did that she turned his photograph to the wall and left it that way until she judged he had redeemed himself.[16]

16. I read about a Michigan woman who said her grandparents were devout Christians and they had a painting of the Last Supper hanging in their front

Radio introduced other American voices to the heated debates of the time. One oddly seductive voice belonged to Huey Pierce Long, Jr. whose nickname, "The Kingfish," was borrowed from the popular radio program, *Amos 'n Andy*. After serving two terms as governor of Louisiana, Long was elected to the United States Senate where he served from 1932 to 1935.

Mythos and *logos* knowing all rolled into one, Huey Long began his working life as a traveling salesman and an auctioneer with the gift of gab. He later studied law, much of it on his own, and successfully passed the state's bar exam. He subsequently made a name for himself battling the large utilities and petroleum interests that had controlled Louisiana politics for generations. With his intuitive grasp of the nature of *mythos* knowing, he made himself beloved by illiterate farmers and common laborers, convincing them that he was one of their own while, at the same time, using his formidable *logos* skills to run rings around the power elite and their cronies in the state legislature. He built sorely needed roads, bridges, hospitals, schools, and other government buildings. He also made sure children received free textbooks, thus promoting *logos* knowing in the next generation.

But his trump card was his talent for using the new *mythos-knowing* medium of radio. The microphone loved his voice, its energy and cadence, as well as his homespun humor and ability to frame political issues along partisan, tribal lines. He knew how stir up an audience, and as his popularity soared he

---

parlor. It was the custom during harvest time back then for families to follow the threshing machine from one farm to the next, spending the night at whichever farm they were at when the sun went down. Then they would eat a communal supper followed by the musicians taking out their fiddles and banjos. Someone would roll the carpet back and everyone would dance. So this woman's grandmother, not wanting to offend Jesus, turned the painting toward the wall until the dance was over. I guess Roosevelt and the Savior fell into the same league in the eyes of some folk.

began to set his sights on the White House. How he might have performed as president, however, will never be known because he was gunned down by the son-in-law of a political rival on a warm September evening inside the state capitol in Baton Rouge, a building Long had worked tirelessly for years to build, a modern-day temple for the *logos*-knowing business of governance.

Other moths besides would-be monarchs were attracted to the light of the new communication mediums. A Catholic priest named Father Charles Coughlin began preaching on the radio in 1926 after the Klu Klux Klan burned a cross on the front yard of his Michigan church. Soon radio stations were carrying his hour-long broadcasts across the country, reaching an audience of forty million at the height of his popularity. An early supporter of Franklin Roosevelt, Fr. Coughlin coined the famous political power phrases, "Roosevelt or Ruin" and "The New Deal is Christ's Deal."

Later, however, he became disenchanted with Roosevelt and began attacking the president in his nightly broadcasts. He assailed "capitalists" and "Jewish conspirators" as well, a theme Joseph Goebbels was using to great effect in Germany. During the night of November 9th and 10th, 1938, in what is called Kristallnacht, "the Night of the Broken Glass," the windows of thousands of Jewish businesses and synagogues were smashed and buildings destroyed in cities throughout Germany. Two weeks later Coughlin went on the air to talk about the Christians killed by Marxist Russians, some who were Jewish, concluding, "Jewish persecution only followed after Christians first were persecuted."

As the 1936 election drew nigh, Roosevelt found himself fighting for his political survival. Polls showed his approval rating hovering just below fifty percent. He was besieged by the Republican moneyed interests on the political right who considered him a traitor to his own class and by social progressives such as Huey Long and his popular "share the wealth" organization on the left. Then there was Fr. Coughlin, the "Radio Priest," with his flock of millions, bashing him night after night. With some desperation, Roosevelt turned to the wealthy and influential Joseph Kennedy, a man who had made a major part of his considerable fortune reorganizing movie studios and selling booze. Kennedy, in alliance with Bishop Francis Joseph Spellman of New York, persuaded the Vatican to order Fr. Coughlin off the air. As a further measure, the pope dispatched Cardinal Eugenio Pacelli, the Vatican Secretary of State, to the United States. Once there, the cardinal joined Bishop Spellman on a whirlwind tour of cities with large Catholic populations where they gave speeches urging their audiences to vote for Roosevelt. The strategy worked and Roosevelt was reelected in a landslide victory. It was a case of the traditional *mythos*-knowing institution, the Roman Catholic Church, exercising its authority over an emerging power, the radio. Roosevelt showed his appreciation for Joseph Kennedy's help by appointing him ambassador to England's Court of St. James in 1938. A year later, on the brink of World War II, Cardinal Pacelli ascended to the seat of St. Peter and took the name Pope Pius XII. One of his first official acts was to appoint Francis Spellman the Archbishop of New York.

CHAPTER 8

A Bum Knee and a Five O'clock Shadow

THE *MYTHOS*-HEAVY MEDIUM OF TELEVISION brought forth a new crop of political leaders in the United States. Many historians believe the defining moment in the 1960 presidential campaign was the nationally televised debate between United States senator and war hero John F. Kennedy and the current vice-president, Richard M. Nixon. Before the debate most analysts predicted Nixon would easily win the election given his experience and name recognition. Kennedy was relatively unknown and a Roman Catholic to boot—until then Al Smith of New York was the only Catholic to run for president, and he was defeated in large part because voters feared he would divide his loyalties between the interests of the United States government and those of the Vatican. The same accusations were leveled against Kennedy by up-and-coming media luminaries such as the Reverend Billy Graham, a Christian evangelist and protégé of media magnate William Randolph Hearst.

Furthermore, it did not help that Kennedy's father, Joe Kennedy, who helped Roosevelt win reelection, had become a controversial figure having supported a policy of appeasement with Nazi Germany while serving as ambassador to the United

Kingdom between 1938 and 1940. During the Battle of Britain, as German bombs fell on London, Ambassador Kennedy went so far as to give an interview to the Boston Globe in which he proclaimed, "Democracy is finished in England. It may be here [the United States], too."

This disparaging remark was the final straw for President Roosevelt, who pressured Kennedy into resigning. Now the ambassador's son was striving to become president himself. Thus it was Nixon's election to lose and lose it he did by showing up for the debate on the night of September 26, 1960 wearing an ill-fitted shirt and nursing a sore knee he had injured two weeks prior. The combination of this injury and the constant campaigning had taken its toll on the candidate; he was exhausted and twenty pounds underweight. To compound matters, he forgot to shave and his perpetual "five o'clock shadow" lent his features a slightly sinister cast. He also disdained to use make-up and went before the cameras looking haggard, perspiring under the hot television lights.

The younger John Kennedy, on the other hand, understood the nature of the new electronic medium. He had spent the previous two weeks campaigning in California and was tan and fit. He wore make-up as well, which helped him look both handsome and relaxed.

The results of polls conducted in the days following the debate revealed that the majority of those who listened to the debate on the radio believed Nixon had won, while the majority of those who saw it on television considered Kennedy the winner.

And the whole Camelot thing, of course, was pure *mythos* knowing: Jacqueline in her elegant gowns, Jack in his sailboat, the wind in his hair, a steady hand on the tiller. Movie stars were constantly in and out of the White House, one or more in and out of the president's bed. Kennedy was America's Sun King, the first president born in the twentieth century.

There would be rough weather during his reign, including the Bay of Pigs fiasco and the Cuban Missile Crisis, but he would emerge more Apollo-like after these storm clouds passed. He sailed a sea of national confidence and hope for the future. We were America, far and away the best country in the world, and Jack the Giant-Killer was our leader. But then an assassin's bullet put a stop to the tale in mid-telling. There was no "and they lived happily ever after."

I was in eighth grade when Kennedy was murdered and I vividly remember the collective mourning and self-reflection made possible by television. Our TV set was on from early morning until the test pattern appeared sometime shortly after midnight. We watched Johnson sworn in as president, Jack Ruby kill Lee Harvey Oswald, and little John John salute his father's horse-drawn casket as it made its sad journey down Pennsylvania Avenue. My maternal grandparents lived with us, and when my aunt, uncle, and cousins were not at our house watching the coverage, then we were at their house, every set of eyes glued to the television screen and tearing themselves away only to use the bathroom or grab a sandwich.

And through it all our grief was mediated and tempered by this strange contraption made of vacuum tubes and bits of wire, our transformation into a television family complete. The familiar faces of Walter Cronkite, Marshall Matt Dillon, and Mr. Ed, the talking horse, were all waiting inside that big box in the corner where the bookshelves used to be. All we had to do was turn a dial to let them out.

CHAPTER 9

Next Stop, the Twilight Zone

I WAS BORN IN 1950. Some of my earliest memories include watching the gravel-voiced cowboy Andy Devine get outwitted time and again by a demon frog that appeared and disappeared in a puff of smoke whenever Andy intoned, "Pluck your magic twanger, Froggie." The show was called *Andy's Gang*, and it was both entertaining and disturbingly surreal. I also watched plenty of *Captain Kangaroo* and *Romper Room*. In the latter, the teacher possessed a "magic mirror" that she held up in front of the camera—I have since learned that it was just an empty hoop on a handle—and she would look through it at the children in televisionland and chant:

> *"Romper, bomper, stomper, boo,*
> *Tell me, tell me, tell me, do,*
> *Magic Mirror, tell me today,*
> *Have all my friends had fun at play?"*

As I got a little older, I watched *Sergeant Preston of the Yukon* and *Father Knows Best*. Later still, *Gunsmoke* and *The Man from U.N.C.L.E.* commanded my attention. I will spare you the tedium of listing all the shows I watched regularly, though many live vividly in my imagination to this day.

On Saturday afternoons, my mother drove me downtown to the Fabian movie theater two blocks from city hall and dropped me off. The sidewalk in front was mobbed with other unsupervised children, and we lined up to get our tickets, stopped at the candy counter for popcorn and a box of Good and Plenty, and then ran down the aisle looking for an empty seat. The matinee always started with a couple of cartoons, *Looney Tunes* if we were lucky, followed by the feature: a western adventure, perhaps, like *The Alamo*, or a science fiction flick like *Forbidden Planet*, or maybe a scary movie like *The Pit and the Pendulum* starring Vincent Price.

The Saturday matinee was a tribal ritual for the children of my generation. With no adults around to scold us, we baby-boomers yelled encouragement and warnings to the actors on the big screen, shot at the rustlers with our pointed fingers, pulled our jackets over our heads as the Man from Planet X came rising up out of the swamp fog, his head little more than an emaciated skull inside the glass bowl of his space helmet. We got bubble gum stuck to the bottoms of our Keds and the kids from the projects poured popcorn and sometimes 7-Up down on us from the balcony; it was great, chaotic fun without an insurance adjuster or public health official in sight.

I sometimes feel a pang of sympathy for the people who ran the theaters back then and the pandemonium they had to put up with each Saturday afternoon, especially when the projector broke down and all the kids started chanting and stomping their feet in unison until the building shook. "We want the movie! We want the movie!" Or when the film got jammed at the most

exciting part in the story and we watched it burn and bubble
away on the screen like the Blob come back to life.

Watching television was also a big part of our family life. My
father died of polio when I was one year old and my mother,
who never remarried, worked as a high school history teacher
and later as a college administrator. She did her best to keep us
together as a family and we ate supper each night around the
dinner table where we either talked about our day or debated
the merits of some controversial event in history. My brother
and I would argue one side of a question, such as Lee's decision
to invade Pennsylvania or whether the senators who slew Caesar
were heroes or villains, but then halfway through the debate,
my mother would force us to switch and argue the other side.
Being kids who liked winning, my brother and I made our new
arguments with considerable sincerity and energy. My brother
today is a litigation attorney, and I suspect our dinner debates
were good training for that.

Fridays, however, were the most anticipated night of the
week because it was the one night we all ate supper on little
folding tables in the TV room. Our bill-of-fare, Salisbury steak
smothered in dark gravy or breaded fish sticks with peas on the
side, was provided prepackaged in cleverly sectioned aluminum
trays by a company called Swanson, the repast appropriately
called TV dinners.

Oh, joy of joys, to sit and watch Perry Mason solve a murder
while ladling forkfuls of processed mashed potatoes into my
mouth. We would each vote on who we thought the murderer
was, knowing it was never Perry's client.

After that came the best show ever made for television. It
began with a gyrating, hypnotic cone of concentric black and
white circles that slowly disappeared into the vastness of outer
space as a shimmering cosmic cloud congealed into the words

THE TWILIGHT ZONE, only to shatter into mirrored shards, the camera panning down from the stars to the scene below. All the while, the unhurried, nicotine-cured voice of Rod Serling intoned:

"You are traveling through another dimension, a dimension not only of sight and sound but of mind. A journey into a wondrous land of the imagination. Next stop, the Twilight Zone!"

Years later, when fate led me to become a professional storyteller, I made sure to include tales of the supernatural in my repertoire. I credit this to having watched so many episodes of *The Twilight Zone*.

I pen this personalized portrait of the United States in the middle of the twentieth century to show how the new *mythos*-knowing mediums of television and film transformed our society in unprecedented ways.

My parents were the first in each of their families to go to college. My maternal grandfather had only a third grade education and was functionally illiterate, although he went to exceptional lengths to conceal this embarrassing fact from the rest of us. Throughout the first part of the twentieth century, the majority people in the United States looked to their *mythos* knowing to make sense of the world and their place in it. They lived on farms or worked as laborers and mill hands, cut trees and fished for lobsters and cod, dug coal and built railroads, herded cattle and picked peaches. For the most part, they shared and consumed their stories orally, rather than reading or writing them.

When tens of thousands of men came home after fighting the Second World War, they found a grateful congress had passed the GI Bill that allowed them to attend college for little to no money. Many took advantage of this opportunity, which was fine with most of the *logos*-knowing individuals who directed the country's political and cultural affairs. They foresaw a time when every citizen would go to college to learn how to use and trust their *logos*-knowing faculties, so that eventually the social ills that have plagued humankind since the beginning of time—poverty, racism, and war—would be rationalized into extinction.

Markets would be organized using rational methods and elections would be decided by carefully considering the issues rather than the personalities of the candidates. Reform would do away with the old political machines, where jobs and contracts were awarded based on personal relationships. There would be IQ tests and performance evaluations, promotion lists and standardized pay grades. Parents would even begin rearing their children using sound scientific methods, such as those espoused by the learned and kindly Dr. Spock.

World leaders of the time had duly noted what unbridled *mythos* knowing did to Germany, Japan, Italy, and very nearly the United States. *Logos* knowing was about predictability, whereas *mythos* knowing, from their perspective, was unreliable, overly emotional, and excessively tribal. What the world needed after the Great Depression and World War II, they believed, was calm, ordered thinking, which explains why they put forward someone like Dwight Eisenhower to lead the nation. The former supreme allied commander was an unemotional and efficient organizer, quite unlike the colorful, self-promoting Douglas MacArthur and George Patton. Eisenhower was the *logos*-knowing man for the future, although photographs of him playing golf, that weirdly *mythos* game, were circulated to appease the emotional needs of the electorate.

In 1964, I went to the World's Fair with my eighth grade class from St. Therese's. The fair was held in New York City and the nation's biggest corporations were there to strut their hot new *logos*-knowing ideas and technologies inside imposing exhibit buildings erected specially for the occasion. Dupont, IBM, General Electric, Bell Telephone, Ford, each competed with the others to have the most impressive pavilion. The most entertaining in my 13-year-old opinion belonged to General Motors. It was called the FUTURAMA and we rode in little cars through a series of elaborate three-dimensional representations of what the world of tomorrow would look like, past glistening skyscraper cities with flying cars, luxurious hotels at the bottom of the ocean, everything clean and orderly and high tech—very, very *logos*. But we were ticking time bombs, us kids, only our parents and the designers of FUTURAMA didn't know it yet. They were sure that their children would all grow up and attend fine universities and become doctors and lawyers and CEOs. But a great many of us would reject this future in favor of a decidedly more *mythos*-knowing path. Why? Because for years, since earliest childhood, we had been fed a smorgasbord of rich and tasty *mythos*-knowing entertainments, courtesy of some of the very corporations who expected us to dutifully don our gray flannel suits and support the corporate program when the time came. They little suspected that the maturing of our brains might be altered by those hours and hours of *Lassie* and *Leave it to Beaver, Bonanza* and *Bewitched, Ozzie and Harriet* and *Outer Limits, Howdy Doody* and *Have Gun Will Travel*—not to mention all those spiffy ads with catchy jingles like "Winston tastes good like a cigarette should" and "See the U.S.A. in a Chevrolet."

   These shows, of course, were unadulterated *mythos* and we loved them. We liked how the stories, so abundant in sensory images and sounds, made us *feel*. They fertilized our imaginations and we acted them out in play. How many times did I unhorse one of King John's knights with a well-aimed arrow, mow down a platoon of charging Nazis storm troopers with my trusty Thompson submachine gun, or blast off with Buck Rogers in a fire-belching rocket ship?

Much of what happened culturally and politically in the late sixties I suspect was tied to this shift in emphasis from post-war *logos* knowing to *mythos* knowing. Some of us were called Hippies. Some of us went "back to the land." We "experimented" with illegal drugs that were illegal because the institutions of *logos* knowing said they were, and authorities would put you behind bars if they caught you using them. Again, why? Because the nature of *logos* knowing is to reject on principal anything that cannot be measured and predicted using symbolic representation. *Mythos* knowing, conversely, welcomes anything that expands or intensifies sensation, either physical or psychological. That is why in predominately *mythos*-knowing cultures, drug use is tolerated and in some cases even encouraged, while its use is criminalized in predominately *logos*-knowing societies.

The influence of *logos* grew steadily from the days of the Protestant Reformation in Europe and reached its zenith here in the United States during the early part of the twentieth century when the chief organs of government, religion, education, and cultural expression were led by highly *logos*-trained individuals. The former university president Woodrow Wilson got himself elected president of the United States, and, with the help of Congress and temperance societies around the country, he managed to outlaw the manufacture, transportation, and sale of alcoholic products. Henceforth, Americans would conduct themselves in an orderly fashion. They would become hard working and frugal, kind and supportive to their children, God-fearing, intelligent citizens. Industrialization was the byword and the bishops of industry required a reliable and sober work force. The battles to be fought, and there are always battles to be fought, would no longer be between the adherents of *mythos* and *logos* knowing, between warring families on Lick Mountain, but they would occur between competing *logos*-knowing groups:

the factory and mine owners against organized labor, countries like England and France competing with Germany and Japan for natural resources and markets.

But people will have their *mythos* experiences no matter what the law proscribes. And so people continued to drink throughout Prohibition. Some were shot and killed for it. Others were locked up for making "spirits," an interesting epithet for alcohol that bespeaks its relationship to *mythos* knowing. A few grew rich trading in bootleg booze and used their wealth to become politically influential. Even my grandparents kept their little roadside hamburger stand in New Jersey afloat during the early days of the Great Depression by peddling illegal hard apple cider out the back door to local farmers and railroad workers.

Contemporaneous with Prohibition, Mexican farm workers brought marijuana into the United States, while Indians in the Southwest used peyote in their religious ceremonies and visitors from the Middle East stashed bricks of hashish in their luggage. The elites responded by enacting a raft of new laws to prevent these *mythos*-knowing substances from corrupting the children who were destined to carry the nation into a future of physical and mental perfection.

As with the monastery clock or the printing press, where a society based on one way of knowing creates a medium that inadvertently undermines that very way of knowing, a scientist at a company called Sandoz in Switzerland came up with a substance called lysergic acid (LSD), and boy did that let *mythos* genie out of the bottle.

Taoist teaching holds that if either of the primal powers of creation, the principles of light and darkness, yin and yang, male and female, so severely suppresses the other that a condition of imbalance is created, then the suppressed power will find some way to reassert itself, often causing a period of chaos and even injury to both powers. This was the role LSD played in helping *mythos* knowing to reassert itself, and, in the attendant chaos, some people were damaged, cultural norms radically reimagined, and political realities altered. It was like throwing gasoline onto a smoldering fire.

The glowing embers were already there, a generation's submersion in television and radio, films and rock music. Way up in Minnesota, a young man changed his name to Bob Dylan because he got turned on to blues and hillbilly music listening to late night radio shows broadcast out of New Orleans and Nashville, the electromagnetic signal "skipping" off the ionosphere to emerge from the small speaker of his radio set next to his bed. Nor was he alone. Lots of young people were buying old 78 rpm records of hillbilly bands and deep-throated blues singers. Some traveled from the cities to the Mississippi Delta or up into the Appalachian Mountains to find the people who still played and sang the older, original *mythos* music. The next thing you know, you've got Woodstock and painted Volkswagen buses, astrologers and imported Hindu gurus, Jim Morrison and city kids living in teepees—all very *mythos* knowing: holistic, sensual, tribal, and "in the moment."

A film came out in 1970 that brilliantly captured the growing conflict between *mythos* and *logos* knowing in American society. *Little Big Man* starred Dustin Hoffman as Jack Crabb, a young white boy who survives an Indian attack on his wagon train in the late 1800s. He is subsequently found and raised by a tribe of Cheyenne Indians, only to be later tossed back and forth as happenstance allows between living with white people and the Indians. He sees the advantages and absurdities of both ways of life, but when he experiences the wanton, unprovoked massacre of an Indian village, his heart is sickened. He becomes a hermit. He considers suicide. But then he offers General George Armstrong Custer his services as a scout, accompanying the general and his soldiers into the valley of the Little Bighorn where he knows full well that the Indians will be destroyed them. It's fair to say the movie had a strong impact on me when I was twenty years old. Already focusing my energies on a more *mythos*-knowing lifestyle, the film provided me with a moral and social framework, an emotional and psychological map, for the person I was becoming. If forced to choose, my sympathies lay with the Cheyenne and Old Lodgeskins, Jack Crabb's adopted grandfather and mentor. After many years, Jack returns to the tribe that raised him, and he talks with Old Lodgeskins about what happened:

> **Little Big Man:** *Hello, Grandfather.*
> **Lodgeskins:** *Greetings, my son. Do you want to eat?*
> **Little Big Man:** *Grandfather? What happened to your neck?*
> **Lodgeskins:** *It's a wound. It cut the tunnel through which light travels to the heart.*
> **Little Big Man:** *You're . . . You mean you're blind?*
> **Lodgeskins:** *Oh, no. My eyes still see. But my heart no longer receives it.*
> **Little Big Man:** *How did it happen?*
> **Lodgeskins:** *White men.*
> **Little Big Man:** *Where's Buffalo Wallow Woman?*
> **Lodgeskins:** *Rubbed out. And White Elk Woman, too, and Dirt On The Nose, and High Wolf. And many others.*
> **Little Big Man:** *And Burns Red?*
> **Lodgeskins:** *Yes.*
> **Little Big Man:** *Burns Red In The Sun?*
> **Lodgeskins:** *Rubbed out. His wife, his children. And many more.*
> **Little Big Man:** *Do you hate them? Do you hate the white men now?*
> **Lodgeskins:** *Do you see this fine thing?* (He holds up a scalp and then puts it down) *Do you admire the humanity of it? Because the*

Human Beings, my son, they believe everything is alive. Not only man and animals, but also water, earth, stone. And also the things from them, like that hair. The man from whom this hair came, (Lodgeskins gives a broad smile) *he's bald on the other side, because I now own his scalp. That is the way things are. But the white men, they believe everything is dead: stone, earth, animals, and people— even their own people. If things keep trying to live, white men will rub them out. That is the difference. You will stay with us, my son.*

CHAPTER 10

The New First Estate

TO BETTER UNDERSTAND OUR OWN increasingly *mythos*-knowing age, let us compare the Middle Ages, the last time *mythos* knowing held sway in the management of human affairs, with today. Medieval people went to a church or cathedral to receive their stories; today we go to the cineplex at the mall. We partake of our bread and wine, i.e. our popcorn and soda, while inviting the sacred story to pour in through our senses, bypassing our *logos* filters—our emotions triggered moment-by-moment by the flashing shapes, vivid colors, stunningly realistic sound effects, and the Dolby-encoded multilayered musical score.

In its heyday, the Vatican was a veritable factory for *mythos*-knowing expression, the place where Europe's most talented artists, painters, sculptors, architects, clothiers, jewelers, and musicians went to find work under the direction of the Pope and his retinue, the masters of the medium.

In the twenty-first century, the artists of *mythos* knowing—the cinematographers, scriptwriters, animators, costumers, set designers, and visual effects experts—ply their trades on the back lots of Paramount and Universal Studios. They too serve the masters of the medium.

While visiting Paris several years ago, I toured Sainte Chapelle, which in English means "The Holy Chapel." Sainte Chapelle sits in the courtyard of the Royal Palace and was built by King Louis IX in the mid-thirteenth century to house two of Christendom's most revered relics: Christ's Crown of Thorns and a sliver of the True Cross. The upper chamber of the chapel is constructed almost entirely of stained glass, with slender stone pillars supporting a royal blue vaulted ceiling adorned with golden stars. Lead strips divide the side windows of the chapel into a series of panels that reminded me of the frames of a filmstrip. Each panel illustrates a story from the Bible, beginning with Genesis and continuing up through the New Testament. There are no printed words, just hundreds of colorful visual vignettes that come to life when the sunlight streams through the glass to enter the eye and reach the heart. Pure, unadulterated *mythos* knowing.

As I meandered through the chapel looking at the windows, I noticed a number of life-sized statues on elevated pedestals. There were twelve in all, six on each side, representing the twelve apostles with each holding a staff and cradling a large round object with radiating spokes that looked remarkably like a spool of thirty-five millimeter film.[17]

If you were rich and powerful during the Middle Ages, you avoided rubbing shoulders with the dirty, foul-smelling commoners in the cathedral or local church. Instead, you had a private chapel inside your castle or manor house, complete with an intricately carved marble altar and painted statues. Today if you are rich and powerful, you have a private screening room with a raked floor, plush seating, and discreet lighting. And if

---

17. When a Catholic church is consecrated, twelve small red crosses, six on each side, are painted on the inside walls of the building. Inside Sainte Chapelle, statues of the Apostles hold discs upon which these consecration crosses were painted.

you are really well connected, His Eminence Cardinal Scorsese might drop by to explain the sacred text to your intimate circle of friends and family.

Speaking of cardinals, back in the sixteenth century during the reign of King Henry VIII, Cardinal Wolsey, the son of a butcher and cattle dealer, became one of the most powerful men in England. Through his role as trusted advisor to the king, Wolsey was able to acquire palaces and large tracts of land. Today, media nabob Ted Turner is the largest individual landowner in the United States. So how did Mr. Turner come to acquire nearly two million acres of land—equal in size to the states of Rhode Island and Delaware combined—and enough money that he could pledge to donate a billion dollars to the United Nations? He began by inheriting an outdoor advertising company from his father (who committed suicide when young Ted was just twenty-four) and went on to build a media empire in cable television—the leap from billboards to television screens being a natural progression since both are inherently *mythos*-knowing mediums.

Another interesting comparison between the past and today is the size and elegance of Cardinal Richilieu's 17th century French chateau and the opulent California mansions Oprah Winfrey and Steven Spielberg call home. It is clear to see that the priests and priestesses of mythmaking have made a real comeback.

When the Spanish and French, two societies that spent several centuries fighting off the transition from *mythos* to *logos* knowing that was taking place in other parts of Europe during the Reformation, set out to subjugate the New World, they made sure to send along a cadre of priests and monks to accompany their military forces. A mural inside the National Capitol building in Mexico City by the Mexican painter Diego Rivera captures this relationship between warrior and mythmaker. A troop of conquistadors armed with fire-spewing muskets and cannons are killing Aztecs, while in the upper corner, a kneeling group of naked natives cling to the robes of a Dominican friar for protection. (Coincidentally, the monk holds aloft a wooden cross that looks very much like a microphone.)

Electronic journalists today wearing Kevlar combat helmets and balancing Sony television cameras on their shoulders are regularly embedded in our military forces in war zones like Iraq and Afghanistan. The job of the embedded electronic reporter is not all that different from what the priests and monks did of old. They help create and disseminate a mythic narrative that justifies the war—stopping the production of weapons of mass destruction, making the world safe for democracy, defeating terrorism—while at the same time serving as a restraining force that can limit the excesses of the soldiers involved.

While George W. Bush and Dick Cheney were preparing to invade Iraq in the wake of 9-11, nearly every major religious organization in the United States, with the exception of the Southern Baptists, came out publicly against the war. The heads of fifty-one Protestant, Orthodox, Catholic, and Evangelical denominations in concert with the president of the National Council of Churches sent a letter to President Bush with the words, "Mr. Hussein poses a threat to his neighbors and to his own people, [but] we nevertheless believe it is wrong, as well as detrimental to U.S. interests, to launch an attack on Iraq."

Pope John Paul II went one better and sent his personal envoy, a longtime friend of the Bush family, to the president's ranch in Crawford, Texas, just days before the invasion. The envoy begged the president not to go forward with his plans.

Bush, however, ignored these pleas and ordered the invasion. To date, the war has resulted in the deaths of hundreds of thousands of Iraqis, many of them civilians. As for the coalition forces, thousands of soldiers died and tens of thousands more returned home wounded in body and mind. All but 139 coalition deaths occurred after Bush's *mythos*-knowing "mission accomplished" photo-op onboard the U.S.S. Lincoln.

In the end, it was the support of FOX News, Clear Channel, and other media outlets, our new mythmaking institutions, that enabled Bush to sustain the invasion politically and even win reelection despite the fact that the primary justification for the war, the elimination of weapons of mass destruction, turned out to be a fiction.

It is illuminating also to note that Italy materially supported the invasion effort and contributed troops for the occupation despite the Pope's opposition. Furthermore, poll results consistently indicated that Italians were opposed the invasion of Iraq by an overwhelming percentage. In February of 2003, the largest antiwar rally in human history took place in Rome, which, according to the Guinness Book of Records, involved over three million protestors.

Despite this opposition, the Italian government joined "the coalition of the willing." Given the influence of the Catholic Church in Italy, this is surprising until you realize that the then conservative prime minister, Silvio Berlusconi, a close Bush ally, is also one of the largest media owners in Europe, owning three television channels, the leading Italian advertising and public relations firm, and the largest publishing house in Italy. He likewise owns film production and home video distribution companies and A.C. Milan, one of Italy's most successful soccer franchises—and his brother owns the newspaper *il Giornale*. Using these mythic storytelling tools, Mr. Berlusconi was able to become prime minister, a position that enabled him to further expand his political power because as head-of-state he controlled Italy's public broadcast facilities. He was Italy's second longest-serving prime minister, having held the position on three separate occasions, and was only driven from office after leading Italy to the brink of financial ruin.

Before the Revolution of 1789, the French ordered their society into three estates: the first estate was made up of the clergy, the second, the nobles, and the third, the commoners. Much later, the press began to be viewed and described as the fourth estate. But with the increasing influence of *mythos* knowing in today's society, the fourth estate is now supplanting the first estate, not in terms of content (although there's plenty of talk about God, burning Qur'ans, and the sin of homosexuality going out over the airwaves these days) but in the way in which they function. The electronic press is the new clergy, and as such they legitimize the rulers.

During a Medieval coronation, an archbishop placed the crown on a warlord's head and everyone accepted the warlord as king. Today, the election commission may certify a winner of an election; the Supreme Court may even intervene with a ruling as it did in the Bush-Gore election in 2000, but the people do not accept the outcome until the media confirms it.

Imagine for a moment what would have happened if the major news broadcast outlets had refused to accept the unverified vote count in Florida. What if, for instance, NBC, CBS, ABC, CNN, PBS, and MSNBC refused to go along with the Supreme Court ruling, refused to send their production trucks to Washington for the inauguration, refused to broadcast the swearing-in ceremony. What if, instead, they broadcasted that Al Gore was the rightful new president? What might have happened? Would people have accepted George Bush as president just because an army sound truck drove through their neighborhood blaring out the words: "George W. Bush is president of the United States by order of the Supreme Court. I repeat..." if at the same time, they were being told on television and radio that someone else was president? How would the electorate have reacted if soldiers had taken over the radio and television stations, arrested the likes of Peter Jennings, Diane Sawyer, Tom Brokaw, Judy Woodruff, and Dan Rather? There might have been serious trouble: massed protests, a tax revolt, military desertions, even armed resistance.

Now imagine a different scenario: one in which the leaders of the old-line churches, the Lutherans, Presbyterians, Methodists, Unitarians, Buddhists, even the Catholics, refused to accept the court-ordered election results. What if they preached from their pulpits across the country a call to resist the "official" government? There might have been confusion and protests for some weeks, but it is difficult to imagine a church-inspired civil war, which we can imagine happening had the broadcast media failed to legitimize the Bush government.

This is the kind of first estate power the electronic media enjoys today, and that is why during any coup-d'état or popular revolution, the first order of business is to seize the nation's broadcast facilities.

Viewed in this light, the media mogul Silvio Berlusconi was the *de facto* pope in Italy, a man with enough political juice to take an unwilling nation to war and still get reelected. The white-suited elderly gentleman in the Vatican was loved and venerated, but he could do nothing to stop the Iraq War because he had been effectively supplanted.

Another thought for consideration: In late 2001, the SISMI, the Italian military intelligence service, sent the CIA a set of documents that purported to prove that Saddam Hussein was attempting to build weapons of mass destruction. These critical documents appeared to confirm the fact that Hussein had tried to purchase "yellow cake" uranium from Niger for his nuclear bomb program. The CIA, under significant pressure from the White House, failed to fully investigate the veracity of these documents even though they turned out to be rather crude forgeries. Perhaps there are echoes here of the secret machinations of the medieval Vatican court at its most corrupt, doling out information and disinformation to this king and that, playing one warlord against another, always with an eye to increasing its power; only in this case, it was the Berlusconi government that provided the Bush administration with the justification it needed to go to war.

I happened to make these comments about Italy and the Iraq War during a presentation I gave to members of the American Leadership Council at their annual retreat at a resort in northern California four days after George Bush defeated John Kerry in the 2004 election. At the follow-up reception a man in a suit and tie came up and introduced himself as a Catholic monsignor.

"I have something I want to say to you," he said, his pale blue eyes boring into mine.

To be honest, I was caught off guard. I didn't realize there were any priests in the audience, and I could feel my Catholic upbringing kicking in. Had I not just said that the Catholic Church was no longer in the game when it came to real political influence? I expected now to be corrected.

Instead, a wry smile stole across the priest's features revealing the Irish temperament beneath—I suspect he wound me up on purpose.

"You know," he said, "we sold the bishop's mansion in Sacramento a few years ago, and the first thing the new owner did was convert the chapel into a private screening room. From where we sit, what you said makes perfect sense."

Returning to our comparisons of Europe's *mythos*-knowing Middle Ages to the *mythos* knowing of today, it is interesting to consider holy relics. It was common once for cities to build impressive churches and cathedrals solely for the purpose of housing holy relics. In addition to Sainte Chapelle in Paris, which was built to house the Crown of Thorns and a piece of the Holy Cross, St. Mark's Basilica in Venice was built to hold the relics of Mark the Evangelist that Venetian merchants stole from the citizens of Alexandria. The basilica also contains the iron chains that allegedly bound St. Peter in his prison cell in Rome before he was executed.

Today, we have our own sacred relics. In 2000 Paul Allen, the cofounder of Microsoft, built a 140,000 square foot museum called the Experience Music Project in Seattle in order to house such items as a broken fragment of the Fender Stratocaster that Jimmy Hendrix burned and then smashed at the Monterey Pop Festival in 1967. The museum, designed by renowned architect Frank O. Gehry, is dedicated to rock and roll music and science fiction, respectively enshrining with Jimmy's guitar and the black helmet worn by Darth Vader, a sinister relic of the George Lucas' evil empire.

Buying and selling holy relics was big business throughout the Medieval Period, just as movie props fetch outrageous prices and are coveted treasures today. The veil of Veronica, for instance, was a top-seller in the fourteenth century, while the Spiderman mask worn by the actor Tobey Maguire was sold at auction in 2008 for tens of thousands of dollars. Interestingly, the last time Dorothy's ruby slippers came under the auctioneer's hammer, they sold for $666,000, an amount that must have spurred speculation among some End Times Christians.

One of the most sought after relics in history, the "Holy Lance" or "Spear of Destiny," is believed to be the spear used by a Roman centurion to pierce the side of Christ as He hung upon the cross. According to legend, whoever possesses the spear will always be victorious in battle. For this reason, Adolph Hitler, a true *mythos*-knowing individual, made sure that the spear was sent immediately to Nuremberg for safekeeping after it was seized from a museum in Vienna during the 1938 invasion of Austria. The spear was later liberated by Allied forces just hours before Hitler committed suicide, events that also accord with the legend, which claims the ruler will die once the spear is lost. The 1981 Stephen Spielberg film *Raiders of the Lost Ark* was inspired by this strange real-life tale.

It may be we regard Luke Skywalker's light saber in our own time in much the same way, as an object possessed of magical powers and therefore worthy of special consideration. An example of this was the decision by NASA to place the original light saber onboard the space shuttle Discovery and send it into orbit for two weeks as their way of celebrating the 25th anniversary of the first *Star Wars* film. It takes a pretty penny to send any object into outer space, and scientists from around the world are lined up in hopes of getting their pet research projects included in a space mission. And yet, the heads of NASA, men of high intelligence and standing in society, chose to honor a movie prop made out of plastic and a couple dabs of paint by sending it into outer space. That is the power of *mythos* at work.

From 1979 to 1985, I served as the founding director of the Youth Museum of Southern West Virginia, and I experienced first-hand the changing nature of museums from what I considered *logos*-knowing institutions into more *mythos*-knowing institutions. The museums of my childhood were, like libraries back then, quiet, orderly places with a surfeit of text to read about the objects on display. I would walk slowly from one display case to the next, almost always moving from left to right like letters on a page, scrutinizing each object for its own sake as *logos* knowing does when reducing things to their component parts.

In many museums today, you will find that interactive audio and video aides have replaced informative text. Hands-on replicas take the place of genuine artifacts so people can use their sense of touch, and many museums now feature IMAX theaters and other *mythos*-enhancing technologies.[18]

Children's museums are not only popular with young people, but they are popular with adults as well. Some years ago, the Boston Children's Museum needed to move out of its original home in an old Victorian house; they had so many visitors they needed more room. At the same time, a popular transportation museum in Boston also wanted to expand. So the two museums, working with the city, decided to build their new facilities next to each other on the waterfront near the moorage for a replica of the Tea Party ship.

Everyone involved in the project thought this was a great solution. What happened, however, came as something of a shock. Attendance at the transportation museum fell off dramatically and eventually the museum had to shutter its doors. The reason for its demise was that people both young and old chose to visit the children's museum first. That museum was large and contained a number of exciting interactive exhibits including "grandma's house," a full-scale three-story Victorian house cut in half. So by the time the visitors finished with the

18. I recently came across an article in the New York Times with the heading: A MUSEUM DISPLAY OF GALILEO, THE HERETIC, HAS A SAINTLY FEEL. The story reports that the History of Science Museum in Florence, Italy, has begun exhibiting recently recovered bones from the inventor's body, three fingers and a "gnarly molar sliced from his corpse nearly a century after he died." The director of the museum justified the decision saying, "He's a hero and martyr to science."

Given that Galileo is regarded as a paragon of *logos*-knowing, the antithesis of superstition and ignorance, this honoring of his bones as saintly relics doesn't make sense. It only begins to make sense when we see that the modern museum is increasingly a medium of *mythos*-knowing.

children's museum, they were simply too exhausted to go next door to the transportation museum, even if that had been their original plan. The days of the traditional *logos*-knowing museum are numbered, thus the twelve-story IMAX showing feature films; it's good for business.

A while back, I visited the American Museum of Natural History in New York City with some friends. One of the first exhibits to draw my attention was a large meteorite that ancient people believed was hurled to earth by the gods. Before setting out, native hunters would petition divine assistance by dipping the tips of their spears into the rainwater that pooled in the meteorite's cup-like depressions.

We were ushered into a huge dome to see an audiovisual presentation about the beginning of the universe. The lights went down and the high-fidelity speakers came alive with the sonorous and recognizable voice of the poet Maya Angelou who proceeded to tell us the story of the Big Bang as galaxies whirled, stars exploded, and planets collided all around us. It was an informative and entertaining presentation, but I was puzzled. Why had the exhibit designers chosen a poet to provide the narration? I would have understood if they'd hired an actor like Meryl Streep or James Earl Jones—another audiovisual exhibit featured the voice of Robert Redford—but instead they had hired Maya Angelou.

I have always considered the Big Bang theory a *logos*-knowing construction, an earnest attempt by the rational mind to explain the nature of Reality. According to the theory, as I understand it, in the beginning there was a tiny ball of matter, so dense and infinitesimally small as to be practically nonexistent. Then there was a humongous explosion that sprayed matter in every direction, each particle picking up speed as it raced outward into the void. At some point, the theory suggests, this matter will slow down and reverse direction. It will then contract back into a tiny, tiny ball only to explode again. Ad infinitum.

As scientific theories go, the Big Bang has its merits, although there are physicists today who are moving away from it. But as a story, it does precious little to engage the imagination. Compare the Big Bang with any of the thousands of creation myths found amongst pre-industrial people around the world and you will see what I mean. Some members of the Iroquois tribe, for instance, believed that the world was originally just water but that deep under the waves there lived a great turtle. One day turtle decided to float up to the surface carrying on the back of his shell a big glob of muck, which became the land from which grasses and trees grow. Sometimes, though, Turtle gets restless and moves; that is what we call an earthquake—it is the great Turtle trying to get comfortable.

To the *logos* mind such stories are absurd fabrications. Clearly we do not live on the back of a turtle. Or as the "square-coated, square-legged, square-shouldered" character Thomas Gradgrind proclaims in the opening lines of Dickens' *Hard Times*:

"NOW, what I want is, Facts. Teach these boys and girls nothing but Facts. Facts alone are wanted in life. Plant nothing else, and root out everything else. You can only form the minds of reasoning animals upon Facts: nothing else will ever be of any service to them."

Enter poetry whose job as a medium is to describe metaphorically what cannot be described in any other way. The Big Bang theory sounds great on the surface, but it does not tell us where the little ball of matter came from, why it suddenly blew up, and what will bring it back together again. It can't even explain what matter is. Pal around with a couple of quantum physicists for a day or two and pretty soon you will realize how little you *do* know. They will talk about particles of matter turning into waves and then back into particles, but not really, only potentially, it depends on how you observe the particles, or the waves. Then there is dark matter and dark energy neither of which can we perceive with our physical senses, and yet, depending on which physicist you talk to, make up together between sixty-five and ninety-five percent of everything that is. And how do they know this? By observing the effects of gravity on what we can perceive and how the stuff that was inside the little ball continues to speed up rather than slow down the further it gets from the source of the Big Bang, which to any golfer or baseball player makes no sense at all.

So you have the Big Bang, a theory that, in fact, tells us very little. At least the Great Turtle legend gives the heart something to work with, like the hunters putting their spear tips into the little puddles of water in the rock that the Creator threw down from heaven.

But there was none of this *mythos* knowing in the text of Maya Angelou's narration. This made me wonder if at some point the museum curators realized they needed to inject some serious *mythos* energy into their presentation. They began by installing ultra high-tech projectors and loudspeakers and doubled down by relying on the "medium" of *mythos*, the recognizable timbre and cadence of Ms. Angelou's voice, not the words, to do the rest.

This use of a celebrity narrator illustrates another difference between *mythos* and *logos* knowing. In a predominately *logos*-knowing culture, true authority is bestowed and withdrawn by institutions. Along with that authority, the *logos*-knowing institution grants a title to the recipient: Mr. Robert Smith becomes Captain Robert Smith, or Dr. Robert Smith, or the right honorable Robert Smith, or Robert Smith, president and CEO.

In a traditional *mythos*-based culture, however, authority comes from one's personal aura, one's soul energy—or as a Sioux might say, one's medicine. That translates today into charisma, being well known and celebrated. The organs of *mythos* knowing pay as much attention to what Lindsay Lohan or Donald Trump say or do as they do the words or actions of Vice-President Biden or Speaker of the House John Boehner. They realize that the content of a person's words or actions are not nearly as important as the elusive *mythos* quality that can command the media spotlight.

Chapter 11

But Beware the Dark Side

BOTH WAYS OF KNOWING HAVE MUCH to recommend them. *Logos* knowing opens the world of nature, reveals her secrets and delights, helps us discover new medicines to alleviate physical suffering, cultivate hybrid crops to feed the hungry, and even launch spaceships to explore distant planets. We can read the thoughts of those who came before us, and set down our own for those who are yet to come.

Our *mythos* knowing helps us feel connected to the world and to each other. It helps us experience the marvels of creation as a whole, not merely as a drawer full of parts.

But history has shown that each way of knowing has a corresponding dark side, a nod to the unavoidable paradox of Reality, the soul-arresting visage of Medusa; all that is good carries within it the potential for its own destruction.

By itself, *logos* knowing possesses the remarkable virtue of breaking the world into its component parts. But in so doing, *logos* loses the ability to perceive and appreciate the interconnected whole, to understand how a set of actions focused on a single part might adversely affect the rest. *Logos* knowing can invent vaccines to prevent polio, the disease that claimed my father's life, while at the same time manufacturing tens of thousands of hydrogen bombs, enough to destroy not only human life but most of the life on Earth. *Logos* knowing reaches down into the earth to extract the remains of ancient flora to burn them for electricity and to power motorized vehicles, while simultaneously filling the air with poisons like sulfur and nitrogen oxides, mercury, and an overabundance of carbon dioxide. These are the dark sides of *logos* knowing: an intense clarity that paradoxically can result in a unique kind of blindness, a reverence for efficiency that can lead to a decision to site six nuclear reactors next to each other in the path of a potential tsunami, a fierce determination to maximize profits at the human cost of destroying communities, and the meticulous parsing of a dozen words in a two-hundred and twenty year old document by nine judges that allows obscene sums of money to corrupt a political system that serves over three hundred and fifty million people.

As for *mythos* knowing, we have already seen how it lacks the tools of discernment, how it cannot identify and protect itself from the charlatan and hypocrite. Furthermore, in its yearning for sensation, its desire for connection, *mythos* knowing is highly prone to tribalism. It is one thing to want to feel connected to others, but for those connections to generate the sensation of genuine involvement and belonging, it is necessary to join a relatively small group. Affiliation with large groups is more or less an abstract experience, like the modern nation-state. There may be financial, professional, or self-protecting reasons for joining such a group, but it is difficult for the *mythos*-knowing part of the brain to experience this kind of involvement as something real, as a palpable sensation. By comparison, sitting in the stands at a baseball or football game and cheering for your team helps you feel connected not just to the team but also to your fellow fans. You sit in a church, synagogue, or mosque and you feel connected not only to a higher power but also to those around you. They are members of your clan. They are your people.

The same holds true for people who cover their skin with tattoos, ride Harleys, attend Star Trek conventions, serve on the boards of natural food co-ops, go mushroom hunting, dress up like Civil War soldiers, attend political rallies, sing in community choirs, and play in golf leagues. These are all to one extent or another tribal groups and being a part of one is highly appealing to the *mythos*-knowing side of our natures. Since we are fast becoming a *mythos*-knowing society, the number of tribal groups is expanding significantly, perhaps exponentially. Just consider the volume of magazines on display at your local Barnes and Noble bookstore. There are magazines for runners, gourmets, computer programmers, antique collectors, gardeners, car enthusiasts, writers—the list is long and varied. Meanwhile, there is an entire online universe of listservs and other social networks catering to almost any subject imaginable.

As recently as a generation or two ago the United States was a more cohesive nation than it is today. There were serious divisions, especially when it came to race and the plight of Native Americans, but among immigrants, especially those of European descent, there was a concerted effort to identify with the nation as a whole. Nationhood is a *logos* construction providing numerous benefits for the citizenry, including a common currency, codified laws, freedom of movement within the state, and a military for national defense. But there must also be strong mythic themes to engender the feeling of being an American, which is why we celebrate sacred "feast" days such as the 4th of July and Thanksgiving and honor the birthdays of "saints" such as Washington, Lincoln, and Martin Luther King. We make pilgrimages to holy sites, to Plymouth Rock, the Alamo, and Ellis Island, revere holy statues such as the Lincoln

Memorial, the Statue of Liberty, and Mount Rushmore—and holy relics such as the Liberty Bell and the original Declaration of Independence.

In days past, children were all taught to recite certain sacred texts from memory. These included the "Gettysburg Address" and "The Midnight Ride of Paul Revere." They were likewise taught to sing hymns such as "The Star Spangled Banner" and "America the Beautiful."

Even the architecture of many of our nation's government buildings, courthouses, schools, and public libraries, were inspired by the ancient temples of Greek and Roman gods in order to appeal to *mythos*-knowing's desire to feel connected, to identify with the whole.

Perhaps all of this—the national holidays, songs, and shrines—seems simple and quaint to us now, but the nature and function of myth, the polished shield of Perseus, is to provide assurance that our lives and actions have meaning. The burgeoning Tea Party movement gives expression to a deep impulse to return to the old religion of national identity by invoking a potent mix of mythic symbols buried deep within the collective national psyche. Members wear tri-cornered hats, ring town crier bells, and wave flags emblazoned with the coiled figure of a rattlesnake and the words, "Don't tread on me." The irony, however, is that what many Tea Partiers want is to more or less dismantle the *logos*-knowing creature called the federal government, believing it has grown too big and indifferent to the rights of individuals.

In much of the industrialized world, relatively small groups are cropping up comprised of individuals whose loyalties are more to the group than the society as a whole. For years our nation has been at war in Iraq and Afghanistan, and yet the great majority of Americans feel little connection to these wars beyond their apparent negative effects on the economy and level of government services. Not being personally connected to the military, they lack the "sense" that these wars have anything to do with them. It is rather the military tribe, along with those who work for private security firms and defense contractors, who are fighting the wars, as it is the right-to-lifers who are fighting to outlaw abortion, Green Peace activists who want to stop the Japanese from killing all the whales, and Occupy Wall Street protestors who are trying to raise public awareness about growing wealth inequality in our country. Again, we see a paradox because this cultural and political fragmentation is largely a by-product of *mythos* knowing being out of balance with *logos* knowing, despite *mythos* knowing's affinity with the whole.

So, when we consider these darker aspects of *mythos* and *logos* knowing, we see tendencies, not inevitabilities. *Logos* can appropriately integrate *mythos* into our lives while keeping the interests of the whole in mind. A person, in other words, can function responsibly as a national citizen while being active in one or more smaller groups. *Mythos* knowing, by the same token, can draw on *logos* knowing to unmask and dethrone the demagogues who would turn us against each other in the name of some imagined difference: the Joseph Goebbels and McCarthys of the world.

We use both parts of our brain, both ways of knowing, to inform and constrain, enrich and modify our behaviors, both as individuals and as a society. Finding, therefore, balanced appropriate uses for *mythos* and *logos* knowing should be one of our primary tasks in life. We should refuse to limit ourselves solely to the pursuit of knowledge, i.e. *logos*, or emotional meaning, i.e. *mythos*, but should with all our will seek wisdom, the blessed marriage between both ways of knowing.

Why do we so often fail in this quest? There may be personal reasons, but there are also powerful vested interests, institutions, and organizations that draw their authority from promoting one way of knowing over the other, praising the one while demonizing the other. They are the entities that hold up mirrors for us to look at. And a few hold up mirrors that are as darkly enchanting as the evil queen's magic mirror in Snow White.

"Mirror, mirror, on the wall, who in the land is fairest of all?"
To which the mirror replies,
"You, my queen, are fairest of all."

But then Snow White appears on the scene and the queen must resort to assassins, disguises, poison, and spells to do away with the competing beauty and her happy-go-lucky tribe of earnest, hardworking dwarves.

Which brings us to the ancient practice of spell casting. As modern people, we take pride in the notion that we have evolved beyond the mystical beliefs of our earliest ancestors. No one casts spells anymore. No one slips a dead mouse under someone's bed to give them nightmares or hides a broom with a broken handle in a neighbor's barn so that his cow gives bloody milk. Only children could possibly believe such tales.

But the truth is the advertising industry is nothing more than one great big spell casting machine. They spend billions of dollars each year identifying, tracking, and manipulating our desires and fears so that we will buy their products, often without really knowing why. We fill our closets to overflowing and then our garages and basements. Soon we are building McMansions to hold all of our "stuff," or renting storage units. And we actually *do* feel better when we buy this model of car or that pair of designer jeans, in large part because we are letting the spells cast by advertisers work their will inside of us.

In 1989, journalist Bill Moyers showed how this kind of spell casting works in politics in a series of public television programs called *The Public Mind*. In the program titled *Leading Questions*, Moyers looked at how techniques used by entertainment executives to judge the popularity of new television shows and feature films were being adopted by political consultants to evaluate candidates and political positions, even how speeches were written and delivered. Here is how it worked: focus groups were given individual hand-held devices wired to a central computer. They were then told to sit back, relax, and watch an episode of a new television show or a video of a candidate giving a speech. They were asked to push a green button whenever they saw or heard something they liked and a red button when they saw or heard something they didn't like. They were told there were no right and wrong answers because the experts who employ this technology, which is called the CONSUMER CHOICE ANALYZER SYSTEM, are not interested in tracking the intellectual response of the audience, but purely the emotional response. The computer then sums the signals from all the handsets and displays the result in the form of a graph that moves up and down depending on how well or how poorly the television show or political candidate is doing with the test audience, enabling the consultants and speechwriters to pinpoint second-by-second what works best, so they can craft their messages accordingly. Some political fundraisers use this technology to determine whether or not a certain candidate should run for office in the first place the same way some television stations use the system to decide which news anchor to hire.

At one point during the program, Bill Moyers talked with Richard Wirthlin, Ronald Reagan's pollster, about the use of focus groups and the CONSUMER CHOICE ANALYZER SYSTEM. The discussion took place while the two men observed a response graph superimposed over a video of Reagan giving the 1988 State of the Union Address to Congress.

> **Moyers**: *As the line rises or falls, the speechwriter can see where her prose soars, or where his ideas plummet.*
>
> **Wirthlin**: *So you can see precisely what words, phrases, ideas, are getting support and which are being rejected.*
>
> **Moyers**: *Right down to the precise words?*
>
> **Wirthlin**: *Yes.*
>
> **Moyers**: *The goal is to discover those "power phrases."*
>
> **Wirthlin**: *It's to fine-tune your communication messages, that is to develop what we call "power phrases" that capture the essence of what you want to communicate in the most compelling and positive way.*
>
> **Reagan**: *It is time—this may be the most radical thing I've said in seven years in this office—it's time for Washington to show a little humility. There are a thousand sparks of genius in fifty states and a thousand communities around the nation. It is time to nurture them and see which ones can catch fire and become guiding lights . . . Let's give the states even more flexibility—*

As it turned out, every time a focus group was shown Reagan's State of the Union address and heard the phrase "a thousand sparks of genius" they pushed the green button. They pushed the green button again when he said, "a thousand communities around the nation," a moment later. Both times the graph jumped up in a positive direction and the pollsters knew they were onto something. For some reason there is something about the word "thousand" that turns people on. The response apparently is primal, it happens below the level of the conscious mind, and this explains is why George H. W. Bush when he hit the campaign trail later that year began talking about a "thousand points of light." Almost every time he gave a speech, whether in front of a group of steel workers or newspaper editors, he would work in his "thousand points of light" line. It became something of a mantra, his most effective "power phrase," despite the fact that hardly anyone knew what he was talking about. One confused citizen, the political cartoonist Garry Trudeau, lampooned Bush repeatedly in his comic strip Doonesbury for the vice-president's continual use of the phrase on the campaign trail.

Bush's political consulting team, however, knew what they were doing. They had learned from their research that every time their candidate uttered the word "thousand," his approval index went up. So Bush kept talking about a "thousand points of light" and, if we take Richard Wirthlin at his word, it was just Bush's way of fine tuning his message to "capture the essence" of what he wanted "to communicate in the most compelling and positive way."

But perhaps this explanation is disingenuous, merely the slab of meat the burglar brings to distract the guard dog. When Reagan read the phrase, "There are a thousand sparks of genius in fifty states and a thousand communities around the nation . . ." it did make sense given his message. He was, after all, talking about a real policy to return more decision-making authority to local governments and communities.

With Bush, however, the phrase "thousand points of light" meant nothing. It was never intended to clarify or strengthen Bush's message because it had ceased to be *content* and had merged into the *medium*. Like a wizard's enchantment, it was added solely to woo the voting public, and his election to the highest office of the land proves that this strategy was effective. At the end of the day, it is hard to argue with success.

A couple of years ago a woman came up to me after a presentation during which I mentioned Bush's "a thousand points of light." "I grew up in Holland," she said in her thick accent, "and I was there when the Nazis took over. I remember how they were always talking about the Thousand Year Reich. It was on the radio, on posters, you heard it everywhere. The Nazis believed they were chosen by God to rule for a thousand years."

I was struck by the coincidence and decided to look a little deeper into the matter. Several religious traditions and other social groups share this fascination with what is called "millennialism." It has been a controversial issue within the Christian Church since its founding. According to one interpretation of The Book of Revelations, Christ will return and rule over the Earth for a thousand years before there is a final battle in which the devil is defeated, and this will be followed by the Day of Judgment. Hitler billed himself as the German messiah and it was only fitting that his party/tribe should rule for a thousand years. The Third Reich, Hitler believed, would become heaven on earth if people would only understand and cooperate.[19]

So, we are left with a question: is it the *idea* of the word "thousand" that affects people, the *content*, in other words, or is it merely the *sound* of the word, the *medium*, that moves us emotionally? Curiously, the English word "thousand" and the German word "tausand" sound quite similar when spoken. In either case, the word is inherently appealing tempting spellcasters of different tribes to employ it in their efforts to sway their audiences.

A last word on spell casting, in relation to our legal system: if you study the health statistics for people who are in the process of being sued for one reason or another, the results are disturbing. They have significantly higher rates of heart attacks,

19. The word "Reich" means realm or empire. The First German Reich refers to the medieval Holy Roman Empire that lasted from 962 to 1806. The Second Reich refers to the modern German empire, which lasted from 1871 until the abdication of Kaiser Wilhelm in 1918 at the end of W.W.I. Despite its boast to rule for a thousand years, Hitler's Third Reich lasted only twelve years.

strokes, elevated blood pressure, irritable bowel syndrome, ulcers, shingles, tooth decay, and premature aging. It does not much matter if the suit is meritorious or frivolous; the negative impact on a person's health is the same. It is the medium and not the content that matters.

Karen Ostrov, Ph.D., is a consultant in Madison, Wisconsin, who works with physicians who are involved in malpractice lawsuits. Here is a note she sent me that she received from the wife of one of her clients.

"It's never really far from our thoughts. It's this weight we feel every day that doesn't go away and can't be solved tomorrow. After so many years in practice with a clean record, now he is being sued for the first time. He feels devastated. I really wonder what the point of such a drawn-out lawsuit is. It will be years before it is settled, and that's robbing us of years of our lives."

So I guess the lesson is: if you want to injure someone, not just get a portion of their money, but physically harm them, then hire a lawyer to cast a spell. Come to think of it, perhaps that is why there are so many dark lawyer jokes.

The young filmmaker George Lucas invited the noted mythologist Joseph Campbell to stay with him for several months at his ranch in northern California while he wrote the scripts for the original three *Star Wars* films. Lucas was getting ready to hold up a very large and shiny new mirror/shield for the world to look at, and he wanted to get the story right, mythologically speaking.

"But beware the dark side," warns the wise Jedi master Yoda. "Anger, fear, aggression. The Dark Side of the Force are they. Easily they flow, quick to you in a fight. If once you start down the Dark Path, forever will it dominate your destiny. Consume you it will."

A word to the wise, as my mother would say.

CHAPTER 12

Lives of the Saints

EXPLORING THE INTERSECTION BETWEEN *mythos* knowing and the world of politics can be both fascinating and troubling. Looking back once more at the Middle Ages, we find that one of the most popular forms of storytelling concerned itself with the lives of Christian saints. Each day of the year had a patron saint whose hardships, miracles, and acts of compassion were dutifully recounted by the faithful. One was the story of St. Brigid of Ireland. Her order of nuns needed land, so she went to the King of Leinster and asked for only as much ground as her cloak would cover. He agreed and her cloak miraculously spread over the whole Curragh.

In today's society, actors and rock stars have become our saints. They may fail as paragons of virtue, but when judged by the influence they exert through their status as saints—it is not the content that matters, what the celebrity stars say and do, but the fact that they are a particular kind of medium in their own right—the parallel with the saints of old is justified.

It is uncanny, for instance, how similar a painting of the sixteenth century St. Teresa of Avila is to a studio photograph of the actress Michelle Pfeiffer. Both share the same angelic features and strike the same pose, their heads turned to the right while their eyes gaze upward into the soft radiance of heavenly light. The stained glass image of St. George set into a pointed stone-arched casement inside a church is nearly identical to a promotional image of Johnny Depp in his costume as Jack Sparrow from the film *Pirates of the Caribbean* standing enclosed in a pointed stone archway, his legs apart, shoulders squared, hands on hips. A painting of St. Anthony cradling a young child in his arms becomes in our day Tom Cruise protecting Dakota Fanning in a promotional shot from the film *War of the Worlds*. And then there is the painting of an armored Joan of Arc boldly standing with her banner, sword, and spear and the image of Angelina Jolie as Lara Croft from the film *Tomb Raider* with a pair of automatic pistols strapped to her tights and the bright glint of holy determination in her eyes.

Consider also three images of Arnold Schwarzenegger taken over several decades. In the first, he is Conan the Barbarian, all glistening pectorals and bulging biceps. In the second, he is the Terminator, a ruthless killing machine holding an assault weapon, his eyes hidden behind dark glasses, and in the third he is the governor of California, dapper in a custom-tailored suit and beaming a smile as he greets the Prime Minister of Australia inside his office in the Capitol building in Sacramento.

This rather remarkable triptych tells the story of how an individual in a progressively *mythos* society can begin his career as a professional bodybuilder and relatively nonverbal star of cheesy B-list films and end up occupying a distinguished and powerful public office.

Nor is California unique in confusing the virtues of the media star/saint in the reel world of film with those necessary for political leadership in the real world. Like intoxicated conventioneers, Minnesotans had their fling with professional wrestler Jesse Ventura and have since moved on to Al Franken, while Tennesseans embraced their Fred Thompson of *Law and Order* fame.[20]

Because of term limits in California, Arnold Schwarzenegger was barred from seeking another term as governor in 2010, which perhaps was just as well since he had little chance of being reelected despite his past boasts to *terminate* California's problems and end the era of "girlie men." And given what happens to historical memory in a *mythos*-knowing culture, the memory of Mr. Schwarzenegger as a public servant will quickly fade from the collective mind of the electorate, as he continues to live on in whatever guise the film industry provides him.

Let me add one last observation that demonstrates where real political power will reside in the future: when Schwarzenegger decided to run for governor of California in 2003 after working behind the scenes to remove the sitting governor, Grey Davis, from office, he announced his candidacy on the Jay Leno show. As my daughter would say, fair enough. He was a professional entertainer, not a member of the political establishment, and the Leno show had a large and loyal following, which meant scads of free publicity. Besides, Jay was his friend, and if the announcement gave the show a ratings boost, so much the better. It was the old warlord/mythmaker dance we have come to know so well in human history.

But when, as governor, it became necessary for Schwarzenegger to name someone to fill the recently vacated position of lieutenant governor, he decided not to make the announcement at a press conference in the governor's office or

---

20. Perhaps a prophetic moment in our new electronic version of the Lives of the Saints was the scene in the 2004 remake of the film, *The Manchurian Candidate*, in which Al Franken plays an electronic journalist who interviews a powerful United States senator played by Meryl Streep. Four years later, despite never having held an elected office, Franken decided to run for the United States Senate himself, defeating the incumbent Norm Coleman by just 225 votes out of nearly 3 million cast.

standing on the steps of the state capitol as might be expected of a paid public servant. Instead, Schwarzenegger returned to the Jay Leno show to announce his choice. He followed this by participating in a comedy skit in which he shouldered a rocket launcher and fired a rocket at Jay's "green" car, reducing it to a ball of flames.

This particular Leno broadcast also featured Lady Gaga singing her single "Bad Romance," and, whether it is coincidence or destiny, big media also placed this feminine mega-celebrity in strange proximity to one of the more significant military scandals of modern times. In 2010, a reporter for *Rolling Stone* magazine spent a month embedded with General Stanley McChrystal and his staff in Afghanistan. During this time, the general and his aides made a number of disparaging remarks about their boss, President Obama, his vice-president, Joe Biden, and other top advisors in the administration. These remarks subsequently made it into the *Rolling Stone* story and the president fired his general, the first wartime general to be forcibly removed from command since Truman fired Douglas MacArthur in 1951 during the Korean War. "Unnamed sources" later alleged in articles in several major newspapers that the general's comments and those of his staff had been "off-the-record," a charge the *Rolling Stone* reporter Michael Hastings denies, claiming he followed all the "ground rules." As Hastings put it during a speech at a luncheon hosted by the American Society of Magazine Editors, "Having a journalist around is like having a pet bear. Most of the time it's really cool, but once in a while it'll bite your hand off."

What is interesting is that even though Mr. Hastings' article had huge political ramifications, the edition of the *Rolling Stone* magazine that featured the McChrystal article considerably downplayed its importance. Instead, *Rolling Stone* hit the stands with a full-page cover of a G-string clad Lady Gaga in profile with a pair of automatic rifles strapped to her breasts. To the left of the photograph the lead headline screamed in a huge font: **LADY GAGA TELLS ALL.** Below was another headline with a slightly smaller font: **DENNIS HOPPER, THE FINAL DAYS.** And at the very bottom of the cover, below two other headlines in progressively smaller fonts was the heading: OBAMA'S GENERAL, WHY HE'S LOSING THE WAR.

At one point in the Lady Gaga interview, the twenty-four year old pop idol made the comment, "Music is a lie. Art is a lie. You have to tell a lie that is so wonderful that your fans make it true."

Athena could not have said it better.

As for General McChrystal, he was a highly trained *logos*-knowing individual, as were the officers who served on his staff. A graduate of West Point, he had an advanced degree from Harvard Kennedy School of Government, and he spent a year at the Council on Foreign Relations. What he failed to grasp, however, was how powerful *mythos*-knowing entities such as *Rolling Stone* magazine really are.

During the interview with Lady Gaga, the reporter pushed for personal information that she refused to divulge, making the comment, "If I say one thing in our interview right now, it will be all over the world the day after it hits the stands. And it would be twisted and turned. And it's like you have to honor some things. Some things are sacred."

That is why Lady Gaga, and not General McChrystal, was the lead story in *Rolling Stone*—not just because she is sexy and outrageous, but because she knows the ways of our electronic, *mythos*-knowing age.

As for the general, smart as he was, he never saw it coming.

The 2008 presidential campaign season was in its early stages while I was trying to sort out this relationship between religious saints and current day celebrities. I began to notice how each serious contender for the nomination seemed to need the endorsement of a movie star "saint." But it couldn't be just any old saint, a John Cusack or Julia Roberts, for instance, or even Martin Sheen (who played the role of president on *The West Wing*). Endorsements and financial contributions from these kind of stars were certainly welcome, but what the candidates *required* was the backing of actors who had become famous playing action heroes.

Mike Huckabee got Chuck Norris to endorse his run for president. He did this by having Norris appear with him on stage while he, Huckabee, was performing with his rock band, Capitol Offense.[21]

Hillary Clinton doesn't play a musical instrument as far as I know, but she did "grok" the action hero/saint thing. Thus during her run for president she invited the actor Samuel L. Jackson to appear with her at campaign functions.[22]

Barack Obama received the endorsement of George Clooney, Matt Damon, and Ben Affleck. He also received the backing of Oprah Winfrey, who, although not an action star, had carved out a unique position within the *mythos*-knowing universe by being both a bishop, one who oversees part of the mythmaking apparatus, and a saint, having acted in films and built a persona

---

21. Bill Clinton and his handlers understood the mythic appeal of music, which is why when he appeared on the late night *Arsenio Hall Show*, he made sure to pull out his saxophone and play "Heartbreak Hotel"—a first for a presidential candidate.

22. Coined by the science fiction writer Robert A. Heinlein in his best-selling 1961 novel *Strangers in a Strange Land*, the word "grok" means to "to understand so thoroughly that the observer becomes a part of the observed—to merge, blend, intermarry, lose identity in group experience. It means almost everything that we mean by religion, philosophy, and science—and it means as little to us (because of our Earthling assumptions) as color means to a blind man." An intriguing new word for our new *mythos*-knowing age, "grok" has even made its way into the Oxford English Dictionary.

as the charismatic host of her own television show.[23]

In 2008, the candidate who ran into trouble finding a suitable action star/saint was John McCain. He first turned to fellow Republican Arnold Schwarzenegger for the saintly blessing, but Schwarzenegger had broken his leg skiing and was hobbling around on crutches. At his second inauguration as governor, the action figure needed help just to get up from his chair. In Franklin Roosevelt's day, the press refrained from photographing the polio-stricken president in any way that might compromise his dignity. That was then. Today it is all out in the open, every wart and pimple. So when early in the primary campaign, the public saw McCain give a speech at a rally with Schwarzenegger standing next to him leaning on crutches, the image of a physically flawed saint did more to damage McCain than promote him.

It also did not help that Schwarzenegger's wife, Maria Shriver, a minor media saint in her own right, appeared at rallies with Michelle Obama and Oprah Winfrey in support of Obama's candidacy, prompting the electorate to ask themselves, "What manly action hero/saint gives his blessing to one warlord while his wife gives her blessing to the other?" It just did not wash and McCain knew it.

So the Arizona Senator took stock of his situation: his father had been an admiral and he himself was an honest-to-God war hero, not some buffed-up, foreign-born actor who only pretends to beat up the bad guys. No, McCain would seek the blessings of real saints, like the Reverend Jerry Falwell in Virginia and the Reverend John Hagee in Texas. It is true McCain did not exactly share their brand of religious belief, but Falwell and

23. The spectacle of James Frey, author of the hugely successful "Oprah pick" memoir *A Million Little Pieces* that turned out later to be mostly a fabrication, appearing on Oprah's show to publicly confess his sins was highly reminiscent of the public confession rituals of the Middle Ages.

Hagee's followers certainly did and maybe some of that "God dust" would rub off on him.

But Falwell, his health waning, would shortly depart this vale of tears, and his support came across as tepid. Of course McCain's earlier characterization of the Moral Majority leader as "an agent of intolerance" and the fact that Mrs. McCain's family owned one of the largest alcohol distribution businesses in the country failed help to help matters much. As for John Hagee's endorsement, this quickly became a public relations nightmare when the pastor's fringe views about Catholics, Iran, and the End Times came to light, and McCain was pressured into disavowing the relationship.

By then, however, McCain was in serious trouble. The campaign was already galloping into the clubhouse turn and he still did not have his saint. So he decided to *make* a saint, which is not as crazy as it sounds. The other candidates had their male action hero/saints, their gorgon-slaying Perseuses and dragon-slaying St. Georges. Well, McCain would trump that with a saint who combined action hero energy—someone who flew through the air in a helicopter to slay, gut, and skin moose—with the fertile Earth Mother: a twenty-first century amalgam of the ancient Greek goddesses Artemis and Demeter.[24]

To accomplish this, he directed his gaze toward the frozen North, to that mysterious terra incognita of the American psyche, the land of the midnight sun that fired the imaginations of Jack London and Robert Service. There he found Sarah Palin with a high-powered Remington resting on one hip and a baby on the other. And what's more, Palin was at home in the electronic temple, having served for a time as a sportscaster at the NBC affiliate KTUU in Anchorage before she got married and jumped into politics.

24. Artemis is the goddess of the hunt and the wilderness while Demeter is the goddess of the harvest and the sanctity of marriage.

And the strategy nearly worked. By offering Sarah Palin the vice-presidential slot on the ticket, McCain resurrected his flagging campaign and he had the poll numbers to prove it.

But high up on Mount Olympus (Beverly Hills to the U.S. Post Office) the other saints closed ranks. Who is this upstart? they asked themselves. Who suddenly made *her* a saint?

One of the first to address the mortals, to warn and instruct them, was St. Matt Damon. He did this by appearing in a special Internet video, a kind of modern-day burning bush with a refresh rate of 75 Hz on most monitors, to remind us that Sarah Palin with her thumb on the button of the nation's nuclear arsenal could call down hellfire upon the earth. "Do you really want to give a false saint like her that much power?" was the troubling question Matt Damon put before us.

Barbara Streisand also made a personal video message saying much the same thing, as did John Cleese. I guess it takes a saint to know a saint, and they were sure Ms. Palin wasn't one.

The outcome of the election, however, was closer than most analysts predicted, despite the fact that the Republicans had taken the country into a ruinous war on trumped-up evidence, mismanaged the war from Day One, and wrecked the national economy in the bargain.

There was just something about that northern beauty that charmed Americans. Perhaps it was her effervescent spirit, those sly, come-hither winks she so generously bestowed on the males in the audience, and her exclusively *mythos*-knowing grasp of history and political realities—all that folksy nonsense about keeping an eye on Vladimir Putin from her front porch. Rather than liabilities, these became her political strengths.

True, there are those who believe Sarah Palin cost John McCain the election. How many *logos*-knowing Republicans, for instance, said to themselves, "Well, if picking a lightweight like Palin to be one heartbeat away from running the most powerful country on earth is the measure of John's judgment, then I won't vote for either of them." This, in fact, is the dilemma the GOP now faces. They have become a party of extremes with highly *logos*-knowing people on one side, Chamber of Commerce types and Heritage Foundation senior fellows, and highly *mythos*-knowing people on the other, Christian evangelicals and libertarian Tea Partiers. A somewhat similar condition existed in Germany in the 1920s. As rival ideological groups fought street battles for political power, the nation's industrialists decided to make common cause with the *mythos*-heavy Nazis, even though many considered Hitler's occult and Aryan super-race theories cracked-brained nonsense. The industrialists believed they could control the Nazis, use them to stabilize the country and the economy so they, the elites, could get on with the business of making money. But the new *mythos*-knowing technologies of radio and film wrecked this plan and allowed Hitler, Goebbels, and the rest of those maniacs to lead their nation and most of the world down the path to perdition.

Let us finish our analysis of Sarah Palin with two thoughts: following the election, John McCain returned to relative obscurity as a senator who would shortly have to fight off a challenge from his own party just to keep his seat. Sarah Palin, on the other hand, went on to a season or two of real political influence. Even after blithely walking away from her responsibilities as the elected governor of Alaska halfway through her term so she could host a television show and campaign for other candidates, she remained a political force to be reckoned with. She wrote a memoir titled *Going Rogue*, with her photo on the cover looking remarkably like a medieval painting of St. Catherine.

Not long after her memoir came out, I was in a bookstore and noticed the cover of *Newsweek* magazine and there she was graced with a heavenly aura about her head and the headline,

SAINT SARAH. Inside the magazine were photos taken at Sarah Palin rallies showing women with their heads bowed in solemn prayer or reaching out like supplicants to touch Saint Sarah's hand or the hem of her garment.

And this made me wonder, why did quitting her job as governor of Alaska not become the political negative many of the pundits predicted? Perhaps the answer is that the true Palin believers saw her decision as proof that God had called her for a higher purpose. For did not Jesus call the fishermen Simon, who was known as Peter, and his brother Andrew, away from their nets so they might follow Him? And did not Jesus call Matthew away from his tax-collecting table, which is what governors do, collect taxes? So too was Sarah Palin called to go into our temples, our radio and television studios, and be God's messenger, to explain the subtle ways of the devil, and "prepare the way" for God's faithful servants to win political office.[25]

When it comes to presidential elections, let us consider some figures. During the 2004 election cycle when George W. Bush ran against John Kerry, the two parties combined spent just over four billion dollars trying to get all of their candidates elected. In 2008, when John McCain ran against Barack Obama, spending on all state and federal races topped ten billion dollars, an increase in spending of six billion dollars in only four years.

The concern voiced most often regarding this unprecedented flood of money coming into our political process is how it corrupts the politicians who receive it. If the pharmaceutical companies, banks, and labor unions contribute such large sums, they must expect something in return. Political donations are

25. The early followers of Jesus fall short in comparison with Sarah Palin in the money-making department, even when adjusted for inflation. Less than a year after leaving her $125,000 a year job as governor, ABC news estimated that Mrs. Palin had amassed over $12 million in royalties, speaking fees, and salary, including a million dollars a year for appearing on Fox News.

essentially bribes, although the word is seldom used.

The larger question, however, when considering the historic shift from *logos* to *mythos* knowing is this: where *is* all the money going? Does it not flow from what are mainly *logos*-knowing institutions, corporations, chambers of commerce, labor unions, and political action committees, into the pockets of *mythos*-knowing entities to pay for radio and television ads, to hire young people to knock on doors and run social networking campaigns on the Internet, to pay for billboard advertising and full-color brochures with lots of photographs showing the candidate doing all kinds of mythic things like visiting factories, touring war zones, or talking with seniors worried about losing their Medicare benefits?

Executives of corporations often bemoan the fact that they have to make large donations if they hope to protect their interests. It's a shakedown operation of massive proportions, which the Citizen's United five-to-four Supreme Court ruling has sent into the stratosphere, the lion's share of the benefits going to the media and their *mythos*-knowing "creatives."

It reminds me of the line from the Gershwin song, "Nice work if you can get it, and you can get it if you try."

CHAPTER 13

The Thrill of Victory, the Agony of Defeat

I RECENTLY INTERVIEWED Mark Moskowitz, a television producer and political consultant who has handled numerous state and national campaigns over the years. Although Mark works primarily for Democratic Party candidates, he has a broad understanding of politics and the role new communication mediums play in determining who gets elected and who doesn't. What was supposed to be an hour-long interview at his home turned into a fascinating and perplexing six-hour conversation, during which he played a number of the political television ads he has produced, pointing out as we watched a variety of persuasive techniques.

Toward the end of the interview, Mark steered the conversation toward the topic of sports and television. He wanted me to understand that early television sports producers, such as the late Frank Chirkinan of CBS, pioneered the techniques that have now become the hallmarks of political coverage. It was the sportscasters and producers who figured out how to get people sitting in the warmth and safety of their living rooms to experience the pulse and excitement of live sports competition. What is more, they got viewers to care deeply enough about what they saw happening on the flickering screen of their television set to tune in again and again.

"They were the guys who taught the rest of us how it's done," Mark told me. "They had the biggest budgets and best equipment back in the early days of television."

In techno-speak, the producers were "early adopters," the first to deploy the newest telephoto lens, shotgun microphones, and wind filters. They built special automated dollies and elevated shooting platforms. In addition to developing and refining the athlete-and-coach interview format, they figured out how to install cameras on a Goodyear blimp.

An intrinsic part of *mythos* knowing is its longing for tribal affiliation. By combining a *mythos*-knowing medium, such as television, with a tribal activity like team sports, the producers were able to induce a state of adrenaline-enhanced team loyalty in their viewers. Nothing mattered so much as watching your team win. With a book, you can always flip to the last pages to find out how it ends. That is not the case with live sports competition. There the thrill is not knowing what will happen next. So everything the sports producers filmed had to be in real time, which meant they had to be prepared: the halfback wasn't going to make his plunge over the right tackle into the end zone a second time. Preparedness required sophisticated planning and lots of redundancy. Like Mark said, they were among the best in the business.

"Spanning the globe to bring you the constant variety of sport. The thrill of victory and the agony of defeat. The human drama of athletic competition. This is ABC's Wide World of Sport."

When I was young, my heart swelled with anticipation the moment I heard that introduction, accompanied by martial music, and watched a lone skier wiping out in an explosion of glistening snow.

Subsequently, the techniques worked out by the "old timers" for sports coverage slowly made their way into political coverage. As a result, political commentators often concern themselves less with the issues and candidates, and focus instead on the strategies employed by the opposing campaigns. When it comes to baseball and football, this makes sense. It really does not matter in the greater scheme of existence if the Boston Red Sox or the New York Yankees win a particular game. Life goes on and the residents of Mudville go to work and raise their families whether or not there is joy in their hearts. But the means employed to win or lose are an understandable and reasonable subject for discussion. Should the manager have brought in a different relief pitcher or substituted a pinch hitter when the bases were loaded?

The trouble began when the live sports production model was adopted whole cloth by political talk shows. Again, if we ignore the content, and focus instead on the staging and color schemes, the music and slick animated graphics, it is difficult to tell the difference between the wrap-up show for *Monday Night Football* and election coverage on FOX and MSNBC. In fact, CNN dubbed their coverage of the 2010 election *The Ballot Bowl*, complete with Super Bowl-inspired pulsing, gleaming text and other computer-generated do-dads twisting and turning on the screen. Clearly, the producers of live sports events and political talk shows are working from the same playbook, ginning up the primal passions of tribalism, the stimulating and unifying dynamic of "us against them."

It is not surprising, then, that shock radio and television host Rush Limbaugh learned his chops while working as director of promotions for the Kansas City Royals from 1979 to 1984. Or that political commentator Keith Olbermann owes his start in broadcasting to sports as well. While still a high school student, Olbermann took a job as the play-by-play announcer for radio station WHTR in Hackley, New York. In college, he served as sports director for WVBR, a student-run commercial radio station. He later worked as a sportscaster for radio station WNEW in New York City and briefly as sports anchor for WCVB-TV in Boston, before heading to Los Angeles, that great *mythos*-knowing factory on the shores of the Pacific, where he worked at KTLA and KCBS and was named best sportscaster by the California Associated Press three times. He then joined ESPN's *SportsCenter* where he worked for five years, winning the Cable ACE award for Best Sportscaster. His next job was with *FOX Sports Net*, where he anchored his own sports news show. According to Olbermann, he was later fired by FOX for reporting on rumors that the News Corporation, which owns FOX, was planning to sell the Los Angeles Dodgers, which (despite a denial by Rupert Murdock) turned out later to be true.

On October 30, 2010, Jon Stewart and Stephen Colbert of *Comedy Central* hosted the *Restore Sanity and/or Fear Rally* on the National Mall in Washington, D.C. Before an estimated live audience of 215,000, Stewart made an impassioned plea to the producers and hosts of cable news shows to lessen the level of rancor and personal attacks that pass for political argument.

This challenge to bring more civility to news coverage and political analysis was taken most seriously at MSNBC, where *Countdown* host Keith Olbermann announced the day after the rally that he would cancel a popular regular segment of his show called "The Worst Person in the World." Two weeks later, however, he reconsidered his decision and asked his viewers to vote on whether or not they wanted him to bring back the segment, a sort of wheels-within-wheels exercise where people cast their vote on how to cover politics, which is in itself about voting. Announcing that over seventy percent of his viewers wanted the segment restored, Olbermann relented and retitled the segment "The Worst Person in the World, Not Really." [26]

Sniping between political show hosts on competing channels has become a staple of cable news programming. The behavior is reminiscent of the fierce rivalry that flared up from time to time between Christian bishops of competing cities during the Middle Ages. Each prelate would attempt to out-God his opponent in the eyes of the faithful through a series of edicts, letters, and sermons, and, if that failed to work, then he would send the problem up the line for the Pope to handle.

Because there is no pope in the realm of media-based mythmaking today, the bishops at FOX, CNN, and MSNBC can pretty much do as they please. During the *Restore Sanity and/or Fear* rally, Stephen Colbert awarded one of his "Fear Awards," a large gold medal showing a naked man running with scissors, to ABC, CBS, Associated Press, the New York Times, and National Public Radio for prohibiting their employees from attending the rally in Washington, even though it was billed as a nonpolitical event. And since no one from these organizations showed up, Colbert presented the medal to a seven-year-old girl, who, when asked if she was afraid to be there, smiled and said, "No."

MSNBC suspended Keith Olbermann indefinitely in November 2010 for making donations to several political candidates, one of whom appeared on his show. (This was confusing since FOX's parent corporation had just given one million dollars to the Republican Governors Association to help fund gubernatorial campaigns across the country.) Two

---

26. FOX News turned a deaf ear to the Stewart/Colbert appeal. This is not a surprise given their highly profitable enterprise. According to the Pew Research Center's Project for Excellence in Journalism, the FOX News Channel earned a profit of $816.3 million in 2010 as compared to MSNBC, which earned $172 million. Combined earnings for CNN and HLN (HeadLine News Network) that are owned by the same parent company were $559.6 million.

days later, however, after receiving thousands of e-mails and telephone calls, the bosses at MSNBC reconsidered their decision and reinstated the popular talk show host. Then in January 2011, while Comcast was in the process of acquiring MSNBC, the cable news channel fired Olbermann who then moved over to Current TV, a new news channel started and run by former vice-president and 2000 Democratic presidential candidate Al Gore.

Meanwhile, National Public Radio fired Juan Williams for comments he made on FOX News. This hasty termination caused much weeping and gnashing of teeth, not merely because it appeared to be an attack on a free and unfettered press, but because the firing was done over the telephone and not in person. This and disparaging comments about members of the Tea Party made by the head of fundraising at NPR during a secretly videotaped luncheon led to the resignation of the network's top news executive, Ellen Weiss.

Another problem in covering political campaigns as if they were sporting events is that each election becomes an all-or-nothing proposition. Unlike the Japanese, who prefer a tie in some sporting events like baseball—they have a lot of people living on a very small island and have learned through bitter experience that it is a better way to get along—Americans demand clear winners and losers. Our sports-reporting language is full of dramatic words like trounced, crushed, drubbed, obliterated, thrashed, routed, massacred, whipped, licked, dusted, conquered, foiled, bested, and smashed. These are not words to inspire restraint. Nor does the attitude that accompanies such jargon make it any easier come the Wednesday after Election Day to work with the opposing party and get anything done. Sadly, "kill the ump" becomes "kill the congresswoman, the judge, the abortion doctor." Again, it is the *mythos*-knowing nature of electronic mediums that not only amplify these combative tendencies but also serve to promote and validate them.

In 2010, I attended a town hall-style meeting hosted by Congressman Adam Smith to discuss the health care bill before Congress. The event was held inside a high school football stadium with the congressman on a small stage on the fifty-yard line facing the stands. People in the Pacific Northwest pride themselves on their civility, but when I arrived at the event, I was greeted by a phalanx of angry protesters waving large placards with a doctored photograph of President Obama sporting a Hitler mustache, images of bloody aborted fetuses, or an assortment of insulting slogans. Whenever Congressman Smith began to speak, the placard holders and their supporters did their best to shout him down. It was chaotic and brought to light my own naïveté; I had heard similar confrontations at other public forums around the country but did not expect to encounter one in my own backyard. The sports stadium is a unique physical space, in that it is designed specifically for ritualistic combat, and perhaps this added to the rude and aggressive behavior of the protesters. There were scores of police officers on hand, and luckily no fights broke out, although I found myself wondering as I headed back to the car how much of the emotional heat arose naturally from the anguished minds of my fellow citizens versus how much was generated by the rhetoric of cable news and talk radio shows. We were not there to debate invading another country, nationalizing our industries, reinstating the military draft, or sending people to concentration camps. We were discussing health care, and the bitter reaction of the protesters seemed wildly disproportionate. Were the protesters the originators of the virus of civic discord, or merely its unwitting carriers?

* * *

I conclude this section on the interplay between sports and politics by looking at the remarkable career of Ronald Reagan. It began in 1932 when he went to work for a radio station that broadcast University of Iowa football games. He was later hired to recreate Chicago Cubs baseball games from inside a radio studio. Back then, play-by-play action was sent by wire to radio stations and printed on a ticker tape like the results of the stock market. Reagan's job was to read the tape and, drawing on his dramatic talent, pretend he was reporting live from the stadium. Once, during the ninth inning of a big game between Chicago and St. Louis with the score tied, the telegraph went dead and Reagan had to improvise. As he later wrote, "There were several other stations broadcasting that game and I knew I'd lose my audience if I told them we lost our telegraph connections so I took a chance. I had [Billy] Jurges hit another foul. Then I had him foul one that only missed being a home run by a foot. I had him foul one back in the stands and took up some time describing the two lads that got in a fight over the ball. I kept on having him foul balls until I was setting a record for a ballplayer hitting successive foul balls and I was getting more than a little scared. Just then my operator started typing. When he passed me the paper I started to giggle—it said: 'Jurges popped out on the first ball pitched.'"

During 1937's baseball spring training in California, Reagan took a screen test for the Warner Brothers film studio, and he was cast as a radio announcer in his first Hollywood film. By the end of his acting career, Reagan had appeared in more than fifty films. One emotionally-charged sports film was *Knute Rockne—All American* starring Pat O'Brien. It told the story of the legendary coach of the Notre Dame University football team who revolutionized the game of football by inventing the forward pass. In the film, Reagan played George Gipp, a gifted athlete who dies from a strep infection. In the deathbed scene, he tells Rockne to "win just one for the Gipper," a nickname that Reagan (and the press) used freely during his presidency.

Not surprisingly, Reagan, the showman, employed his skills in another competitive arena, the presidential debate. On February 25th, 1980, Jon Breen, the managing editor of The *Nashua Telegraph*, moderated a debate between two Republican candidates who were competing in the New Hampshire primary. One was George H. W. Bush, former congressman, ambassador to the United Nations, and director of the C.I.A. The other was Ronald Reagan, a former film and television actor turned politician who served two terms as governor of California. For several days controversy plagued the proposed debate. The Bush campaign had approached the newspaper with the idea of hosting the debate on the Saturday evening before the election. There were seven candidates in all on the Republican ballot in 1980, including Senator Bob Dole of Kansas, Senator Howard Baker of Tennessee, Congressman Phil Crane of Illinois, and former Texas governor John Connally. The last candidate, Republican congressman John Anderson, was running as an independent. The election, however, was down to the wire and only two candidates, Bush and Reagan, had any hope of winning. Bush, who was coming off an upset victory over Reagan in the Iowa caucuses, was leading in the polls by twenty points. He was considered something of a native son in New Hampshire because his father had served two terms as a United States senator for Connecticut, and the Bush family vacationed each summer in nearby Kennebunkport, Maine. If that wasn't enough, many voters considered the sixty-nine year old Reagan too old to assume the mantle of leadership of the free world. If elected, he would be seventy years old when he took office, the oldest president in United States history, and there were rumors he took a nap every day and dyed his hair. Furthermore, Bush, the oilman, had significant experience with international affairs while Reagan was better known for having once starred in a film opposite a chimpanzee named Bonzo.

Given there were few issues of substance dividing the two candidates, the Bush team believed a one-on-one match-up would only amplify their man's youthful vigor and keen intelligence compared to the grandfatherly Reagan. For Reagan, it was his final chance at becoming president. He had run for the GOP nomination in 1972 and again 1976, but each time he came up short. In 1980, despite being heavily favored to win in Iowa, he was soundly defeated. If he lost the New Hampshire election, his candidacy was finished and everyone knew it. In football terms, he needed a "Hail Mary" play.

But a controversy was brewing because the other candidates resented being left out of the debate. Senator Bob Dole, in fact, went so far as to lodge a formal complaint with the Federal Elections Commission, which ruled that since the newspaper had only invited two candidates to participate in the debate they were, in fact, making an illegal contribution to the Bush and Reagan campaigns.

The newspaper responded by asking the two campaigns to pick up the tab for the debate. The amount was only $2,000, a pittance even by 1980s standards, but the Bush campaign here made what would turn out to be a fatal miscalculation. Trusting their candidate would win the upcoming primary handily, they saw no reason to help underwrite the debate. They reasoned that if Reagan wanted one last shot at making his case to the voters of New Hampshire, then he should pay for it.

The Reagan camp jumped at the chance. They foresaw that by ponying up the money for the debate they would become the event sponsor with all the privileges that came with sponsorship, a position Reagan understood well from his years working in television as a shill for General Electric and other corporations.

Thus the stage was set on that wintry Saturday evening, and Jon Breen entered the Nashua High School gymnasium to begin directing the placement of tables and microphones, setting out glasses and pitchers of water, and making last minute changes to his list of questions for the candidates. Even though the debate would not be broadcast live on television, the major networks had sent correspondents and camera crews to film the event just in case something unexpected happened. Everyone knew that unless something dramatic did happen, Bush would sail on to victory in the primary and his party's nomination for president.

The population of New Hampshire in 1980 was just over two million, and Jon Breen was on a first-name basis with most of the state's major political players. But he had never met George Bush or Ronald Reagan; he had only dealt with their campaign staffers. Add to that the presence of nationally known journalists like John Chancellor of NBC News, and it is understandable that the forty-five year old Breen was brimming with nervous excitement and hoping with all his being for a successful event.

Slowly the folding chairs and bleachers in the gymnasium filled with people. Many in the audience carried signs and Breen realized that the overwhelming majority of them were ardent Reagan supporters. This was because Reagan, by paying for the debate, had gained control of the invitation list. The result of this, drawing upon the sports metaphor, was to give Reagan the home field advantage despite Bush's ties to New England. There is nothing, after all, like the boisterous cheers and energetic boos of a crowd to fire up the home team and intimidate the visitors.

Then Reagan himself arrived with his top coaching staff in tow. He manfully strode through the gymnasium on his way to the green room, a converted locker room, all the while smiling and waving to well wishers in the audience or momentarily tilting his head to receive an urgent whispered report from a campaign aide. People clapped and cheered while those in the front rows pushed forward to shake hands with the great man. With no soft surfaces to absorb the sound waves, the noise level inside the gymnasium was deafening. It reminded Breen more of a basketball game between rival schools than a debate where weighty matters of state would shortly be discussed by reasonable and well-intentioned grown men. He was suddenly anxious lest the event somehow spiral out of control. Then one of Reagan's aides approached him to say that Reagan's campaign manager wished to have a word or two out in the hallway. Breen stepped through a door into the hallway where the manager informed him that Reagan had reconsidered his decision to bar the other candidates from the debate. What's more, Reagan had called the candidates that morning and invited them to attend. Now he wanted Breen to make the necessary arrangements, such as providing additional chairs and microphones.

Breen couldn't believe his ears. Surely, Reagan knew it was impossible to make such a major change so late in the game. And besides, the Bush people would most likely take a hike if suddenly informed that it was now a debate between seven candidates, not two. Even the word "debate" would be misleading; it would be little more than a conversational free-for-all.

Breen, no virgin to politics, began to see what was going on: every candidate in a race has a stake in bashing the front-runner and Reagan had invited Dole, Baker, and the others precisely for that reason.

No, Breen informed the campaign manager, it was not possible to include the other candidates at the last minute. They were already seriously behind schedule, the format had been agreed upon for more than a week, the television cameras were in place and ready to roll, and he had already made the final edits to his list of questions. The idea was simply out of the question.

The manager, however, reminded Breen that Reagan was paying the freight, and, if the governor wanted the other candidates participate, then by golly they would.

The minutes ticked by and Breen could sense the audience in the auditorium growing restless; they, like the press, were in the dark as to what was going on. By this point, aides for the Bush campaign had learned about the proposal to include the other candidates and they hurried off to huddle with their quarterback. Word came back; it was up to Breen. It was his call.

Breen glanced at his watch again. They were forty minutes behind schedule and if he did not make a decision, and soon, he would have a riot on his hands.

Once more he told the Reagan camp, "I'm sorry but we can't make changes at this late date. Now let's get the show on the road."

So Breen and the two candidates filed into the gymnasium. Breen went first and sat in the moderator's chair at the center of a long table, followed by Bush who took his assigned chair on the left side of the table. Reagan then entered and took the chair on the right. They were about to start when four more candidates entered the gymnasium: Dole, Baker, Crane, and Anderson. (Connally was campaigning at the other end of the state when he got the call and could not make it to Nashua in time.)

Again Breen was taken off guard; he didn't even know the candidates were in the building, let alone the fact that the Reagan people had stashed them away in an equipment storage room beforehand. Now they were milling around behind him a bit sheepishly without chairs or microphones to use.

Meanwhile, audience members were becoming more vocal in their frustration and Breen tried to calm them by explaining the nature of the problem. One thing he was certain of: he was not going to let Reagan and his California gang hijack the debate. This was New Hampshire. It was a Republican event and Republicans in New Hampshire were conservative, thoughtful people. They believed in rules and proper conduct. They also believed in personal responsibility; you gave your word and you stuck by it.

But as he began to address the crowd, he caught out of the corner of his eye Reagan leaning closer into his microphone. Suddenly Reagan was talking to the audience, complaining about how the other candidates were being shut out of the debate, how that was not fair, and how he, Reagan, had invited them to be a part of the event.

Breen let him speak for several minutes, irritated but also impressed by Reagan skill as a trained orator. Most of the people in the audience, intoxicated by the scent of political testosterone in the air, were yelling, holding up placards, and stamping their feet on the pullout bleachers. It was clear they regarded Breen and the *Telegraph* as the villains of the piece and didn't give a tinker's dam for antiquated notions of protocol; they had come to see a debate, a real knock 'em down and drag 'em out fight, and as far as they were concerned, the more knocks and drags the better.

Breen was hoping Bush would jump in and say something to quiet the audience, but he just sat there looking like the proverbial deer in the headlights. So Breen made several attempts to persuade Reagan to stop talking, but Reagan ignored him. Finally, feeling he had no other choice, Breen directed the soundman to switch off Reagan's microphone.

This was the moment the Reagan campaign had hoped and planned for. Like *Knute Rockne*, John Sears, Reagan's campaign manager, had cooked up his own never-before-seen play. The formation was in place: Reagan on the right wing, the excluded candidates clustered at the center, behind the moderator, and Bush on the left, too far away to see what was coming.

It was time to run the play. In a display of what appeared to be genuine anger at an obvious injustice, Reagan stood up and glared at Breen. He then turned back to the audience, reaching down and grabbing hold of his microphone.

"Is this still on?" he asked to which the delighted crowd yelled back, "Yeah!"

Again Breen told the soundman to turn off the microphone.

As any actor or athlete will tell you, timing is everything. Reagan then delivered a line that would change history.

"I *paid* for this microphone, Mr. Green!" he thundered, his righteous anger mangling the moderator's surname.

The crowd went nuts, hooting and hollering and clapping their hands, while the standing candidates smiled and applauded heartily, the glint of adoration shining in their politically savvy eyes. They realized, as had the media, that something momentous had just occurred. Bush, for his part, just sat there mute wearing his granny glasses like someone who had just had the wind knocked out of him. Everyone in the gymnasium and the millions across the country who would watch the scene on their television sets in the following days knew that Reagan had not only challenged the moderator's authority, he had directly challenged the opposing alpha-male, George H. W. Bush. So what was Bush going to do about it? Apparently nothing. He just sat there waiting for God only knows who to come along and somehow rescue his candidacy.

Or as the journalist Jules Witcover put it later, "Through all this Bush sat woodenly at the debate table, staring straight ahead like a goody-two-shoes in the midst of a college cafeteria food fight."

So that was it. In the time it takes to tie your shoes, Ronald Reagan had been transformed from a tired old man into a dynamic leader. If he could stand up to the media and the rich elite Republican types, the voters now believed, he could stand up to the Russians and any other Communists around the world who ever thought of pushing the U.S. of A. around.

By Sunday morning, the tale of the microphone was the lead story in every newspaper and television news broadcast in the country. Two days later, Reagan handily won the New Hampshire primary in a mythic come-from-behind victory for the Gipper. He then went on to win his party's nomination and the general election, serving two terms as president of the United States.

Most political analysts cite the Nashua debate as the moment Reagan became a national political figure. Even Reagan, when writing his memoir, agreed:

"That winter, a brief and seemingly small event, one lasting only a few seconds, occurred in a high school gymnasium in Nashua, New Hampshire, and I think it helped take me to the White House . . . for some reason my words hit the audience, whose emotions were already worked up, like a sledgehammer. The crowd roared and just went wild. I may have won the debate, the primary—and the nomination—right there."

But there's more to this quintessential yarn than a mere show of unscripted bravado on the part of the candidate. For starters, the American public had been conditioned day in and day out for years to regard the microphone as more than bits of copper wire, steel, and a collection of transistors. Microphones were and are genuine power objects in much the same way that a beaded and feathered ceremonial pipe was a power object to a Sioux war chief, the sacred drum was to a Mongolian shaman, rosary beads were to the nuns at St. Therese's, or the old pigskin was to Knute Rockne. Whoever therefore controls the microphone in a *mythos*-knowing culture is the person with authority. Watch how many high-profile performers handle a microphone on stage: how they grab it boldly with one hand and then with both, how they bring it up so close to their mouth that they appear to kiss it, for in its symbolic form, the microphone is the chalice into which they will pour forth the wine of their souls to renew the soul energy of their adoring fans. For that matter, notice how at most press conferences microphones sprout from the podium like bouquets of exotic flowers; the more important the press conference, the larger the bouquet.

I was once asked to work with incarcerated young men on a project developed by the California Youth Authority called *Young Men as Fathers* that would culminate with participants writing and performing a radio play about how to be a responsible father. Not the most exciting of subjects from their point of view. Nor did it help that I was an aging white guy with the salt and pepper beard, not unlike many of the psychologists and judges they had been forced to deal with over the years. I was not surprised on the first day when I was greeted with a show of universal and exaggerated apathy, eyes heavy lidded or gazing at the floor, legs sprawled out and bodies leaned away. The teacher, a person with unbounded patience, looked at me with sympathy, and I imagined I could hear the words inside her head, "This is not going to go well."

But then my intuition came to the rescue. By luck I had my recording gear with me and with the flair of a magician I reached into the equipment bag and produced a mahogany box. This I opened and removed from its felt-lined interior my prized twelve-hundred dollar large-diaphragm Australian-made vacuum-tube microphone, a device that looks suspiciously in shape and size like a can of dog food, except that in its high-tech brushed-steel enclosure with fine mesh wind screen and gold-sputtered capsule just visible inside, it is really quite handsome. Suddenly, every eye in the room was on me as I told them that I would record them performing their radio plays using this microphone.

A youth in the back of the room, who I later realized was the leader of that broken and stubborn clan, spoke up. "You mean, we can record with that mic if we do what you want?"

"Yes," I said.

The youth thought a moment—in the room silence reigned—and then he shrugged and said, "That's cool." And just like that, I had them all on board. Without consciously intending to, I had tapped into something primal. Driving home later I came up with this explanation: the young men in the juvenile hall were in a perpetual state of war with the *logos*-knowing world, first with teachers, principals, and school psychologists, and later with the police and officers of the court. These agents of the status quo, their *logos*-knowing enemies, each had a power object: the policeman had his nightstick, the judge his gavel. Now here I was, the possessor of a significant *mythos*-knowing power object, offering to let them to use it, a gesture that made us allies and led to the project's great success. I hope they learned something useful. I know I did. I learned how deep the mediums of *mythos* knowing have penetrated the culture and how much influence they wield both consciously and subconsciously.

Ah, but there is a final episode to the Nashua debate saga. An accomplished actor, Reagan often borrowed lines of dialogue from popular Hollywood films, and it turns out his "I paid for this microphone" line was not the spontaneous and original reaction people took it to be. Instead, it seems he lifted it whole cloth from the 1948 Frank Capra film *State of the Union* starring Katherine Hepburn and his old friend Spencer Tracy. In that film, Tracy plays an industrialist who is talked into running for president on the Republican ticket. He begins his campaign determined to tell people the truth about the pressing issues of the day but is corrupted over time by his political handlers. He makes deals with selfish power-hungry politicians and labor union cronies just to get their support. He gives speeches written by back-room operatives rather that those he has written himself. Blinded by ambition, he ignores the advice of his wife and close friends. The emotional climax of the film comes on the eve of the Republican convention when Tracy is about to give a nationally televised speech from his home. The broadcast, in fact, has been paid for by "the nickels and dimes" of his admirers, including their children. The living room is packed with television cameras, sound engineers, news photographers, political hacks, and a crowd of neighbors and other supporters. At the last moment, thanks to his wife, Tracy decides to come clean with the American public. He steps up to the microphone and begins a discourse on the inner workings of the political machine and how he was seduced into betraying his own beliefs. It is classic Frank Capra high drama, and when the director of the broadcast realizes what is going on, he yells at the soundman to switch off Tracy's microphone. A sympathetic newspaper reporter, however, has positioned himself next to the engineer and convinces the man to ignore the order and keep the microphone live. As the director tries to force his way toward the control board, an angry Tracy grabs the microphone stand in one hand and points at the director with the other. "I paid for this broadcast!" he thunders, and the crowd of supporters roars their approval. Then another crony attempts to wrest the microphone away from Tracy but is shamed into retreating, his arm over his face as he turns and flees like Adam driven from the Garden. Again, the crowd yells and applauds.

It is difficult to believe after watching this scene from *State of the Union* that the fictional Tracy speech and the very real fracas in Nashua thirty-two years later are unrelated. The content of each character's actions and ambitions are different, but the defining role the microphone plays as a power object is the same. The medium, after all, is the message.

So this made me wonder, who was in on it? It appeared too perfectly staged to be mere coincidence and I decided to talk to the debate moderator, Jon Breen. Mr. Breen is now in his seventies but vividly remembers what took place that night.

"I had no doubt we'd had a number done on us. Here we felt we had an opportunity to do something worthwhile and the whole thing just got blown away by, I think, the failure of the Bush campaign to be hard-nosed, because for a few minutes, instead of being a debate between Ronald Reagan and George Bush, it was a debate between Ronald Reagan and Jon Breen, and who the hell was Jon Breen? He just happened to be sitting there, interestingly, between the two."

I asked him why he told the sound man to switch off the microphone.

"Governor Reagan was a fine orator and he was just going on and on. And I interrupted him—tried to interrupt him—and he just ignored me.

"How long did this go on?" I asked.

"Probably a couple of minutes but it seemed like an hour," Mr. Breen said with a laugh. "Then I tried to interrupt him once more to explain that we had to start moving things along, and again he just ignored me and continued to talk and it was at that point I turned and looked over at the sound person and asked him to turn off Governor Reagan's microphone. It probably wouldn't have made any difference because when he speaks, the entire audience would have heard him anyway."

As to why the sound man failed to turn off the microphone, Mr. Breen said, "I won't say he was paid by the Reagan campaign; I don't think he was. But I learned later there was a Reagan operative sitting just behind him."

This matches the situation in the *State of the Union* film, except, in the movie, it is a newspaper reporter, not a campaign staffer, who convinces the sound man keep the microphone "live."

Mr. Breen's account also squares with what Craig Shirley, a prominent conservative consultant and close ally of Ronald Reagan, wrote his book *Rendezvous with Destiny*:

"Reagan, the old pro, tapped his microphone. It was already on, because steps had been taken, according to Carmen, to make sure the soundman, Bob Molloy, was under their control."

I concluded my conversation with Mr. Breen by asking him about the debate itself. He told me that after the staged outrage about the microphone, the two candidates gave their opening statements and the debate went forward without any further comment on Reagan's part about letting the other candidates join in. I suspect Dole and company had successfully played their part in the wee melodrama and were no longer needed.

"The debate became an addendum," Mr. Breen said. "There was no content that evening. The debate went on. The two candidates expressed themselves very articulately. However, I had no doubt what was going to appear in next morning's newspapers and on the TV shows. It was going to be The Event and I think since then it's accelerated to where we are now. That might have been a watershed beginning."

I sometimes find myself wondering what our country and the world would be like today had Bush and not Reagan won the

New Hampshire primary and gone on to clinch the Republican nomination. Would Carter have successfully resolved the Iran hostage crisis and beat Bush in the general election? Would the United States be energy independent today and would that have prevented us from going to war in Iraq? Would the Berlin Wall have fallen? Would Bush's son, George W., gone on to become president United States?

Of course, there's no way to answer these questions, because of a few seconds in Nashua one wintry evening that put a former sportscaster and film actor into the White House.

CHAPTER 14

A Great Big Life with a Great Big God

THERE IS A SCENE IN THE 1960 Academy Award-winning film
Elmer Gantry (based on the novel by Sinclair Lewis) during
which a traveling evangelical preacher named Sister Sharon
Falconer and her sidekick, the colorful con-man Elmer, meet
with the church committee of the fictional Midwestern city of
Zenith. Set in the 1930s, the churches of Zenith are struggling,
and the committee chairman, a wealthy businessman and
community booster named George Babbitt, believes an old-
fashioned big tent revival is just what people need to get them
to come back to church.

The meeting commences with a minister on the committee
complaining, "I'm not ashamed to admit our churches are half-
empty. The ballparks are full. So are the races."

Another minister bemoans the fact that his church has not
been painted in eight years, a third that his church needs a new
gymnasium, a fourth that in his neighborhood they are unable
to pay for milk for the needy children.

"Your problem is empty churches, gentlemen," Elmer
Gantry says, "That's your problem."

"That is a fact!" Babbitt agrees.

"The unpleasant fact is that church attendance is falling off everywhere," says bespectacled Bill, Sister Falconer's business manager.

"Yes, and Sister Falconer can fill your churches," Elmer chimes in. "That's why you're here in the first place.

"I always say, if you're sick, call a doctor," intones a smiling Babbitt. He then asks the committee to vote.

"Vote to do what?" asks a disgruntled preacher. "Marry the Church to a three-ring circus? To barkers who say they're messengers of God? Who reduce frightened farmers to howling dogs? All very entertaining, I'm sure."

"We are in competition with the entertainment business," counters Babbitt with the other ministers on the committee nodding in agreement.

"I'm not," the disgruntled preacher argues.

"Then you ought to be," says Babbitt. "How about your bingo games? And how about your baseball games and square dances? Now, ain't that entertainment? What's the difference? It's up to us to make a success out of Christianity, keep the churches full."

"What has religion to do with filling churches?" another minister asks. "Once there were only thirteen Christians in the entire world. Was Christianity a failure? Did God go out of business?"

"Right," says a beaming Babbitt. "Christianity is a going concern, a successful international enterprise. If you boys don't get young people back into church, if you don't keep the train on the tracks, your church boards are gonna find somebody else who will."

The tent revival was a staple of American cultural life for many years, serving as a *mythos* counterbalance to the increasingly *logos*-knowing ways of mainstream Christian Protestantism.

Combining fiery oratory, faith healing, and hours of fervent hymn singing, the revival whipped people into a religious frenzy. Grown men and women wept as they came forward to unburden themselves of their wrongs or shake uncontrollably with joy as they were "washed in the blood." Others entered trances and spoke in tongues.

To the *logos*-knowing sophisticate, the religious tent revival was humbug, a cynical ploy by scoundrels and charlatans to dupe the susceptible and uneducated out of their hard-earned money. But then and now people need *mythos* knowing in their lives and will seek it out. They might paddle a kayak across a lake at sunset, enjoy a chamber music concert, run a 5K race, toast marshmallows in the flames of a campfire, go up in a hot air balloon, or knock a little white ball around a big lawn in a game of golf.

Some individuals, however, crave more intense experiences and technology is only too happy to oblige. There are rock concerts with computer controlled laser light shows to dazzle the eyes, towering stacks of loudspeakers to pound the ears, and fireworks shooting out of skimpy bras and bass guitars held up like erections to excite the sexual senses. There are NASCAR races where people can smell the acrid stench of burning rubber, listen to the chest-thumping roar of supercharged engines, and delight in the flash of bright colors as cars zoom past them. And, of course, there is always the chance of a crash with billowing flames and wailing sirens and the period of waiting to hear if any of the drivers were injured or killed.

In 2008, the Democratic National Committee decided to move the last day of their nominating convention from the 21,000-seat Colorado Convention Center to the open-air 76,000-seat INVESCO Field football stadium in Denver, home of the Denver Broncos. It was time to pull out all the stops and play the *mythos*-knowing organ for all it was worth. This was not the first time the Democrats used an open-air stadium as a venue for a presidential nominating convention; Franklin D. Roosevelt spoke before an audience of 100,000 at Franklin Field in Philadelphia in 1936, and John F. Kennedy addressed 80,000 at the Los Angeles Coliseum in 1960. The principle behind gathering so many people together in one place in support of a presidential ticket is known today as "social proof," the instinctual impulse of people to behave like other people.

Robert Chaldeni, a professor at Arizona State University, has done fascinating research on this subject. In his book *Yes, 50 Scientific Ways To Be Persuasive*, he details his experiments examining our innate tendency to act in concert with what we perceive to be the "wisdom of the crowd." One example he cites was a failed attempt by the staff of the Petrified Forest National Park in Arizona to discourage people from taking away pieces of petrified wood. They tried to do this by putting up a sign informing visitors that some people were picking up petrified wood and, if they did not stop, soon there would not be any petrified wood left. What happened, however, was that the theft of petrified wood expanded substantially because the sign told people that other people were picking up wood—*and maybe they should too*. A similar thing happened to the Internal Revenue Service. They mailed out a warning stating that some people were cheating on their taxes and that IRS agents were intensifying their efforts to catch them. The number of tax evaders was not all that high at the time but the number jumped after the warning went out because it told people that other people were cheating on their taxes.

One interesting experiment to test the efficacy of using social proof to get people to change their behavior involved changing signs in the bathrooms of a large hotel. The old signs encouraged visitors to conserve water and help protect the planet by reusing their towels. But after the researchers replaced these signs with others assuring visitors that many of the other hotel visitors were reusing their towels to help conserve water and protect the planet, the number of people who reused their towels increased dramatically.

That is why the Democrats and the Obama campaign decided to culminate their convention at INVESCO Field. They wanted the television audience to see and hear an enormous crowd of cheering people supporting their candidates. They also encouraged those attending the event to use their cell phones to call or text their families and friends at home to tell them to tune into Obama's speech, turning the stadium into one massive call center.

Furthermore, each speaker was selected and each rally choreographed so that together they built toward an intense emotional crescendo—known by orators since the days of Aristotle as "catharsis"—when Barack Obama strode down the thirty-six-foot long blue-carpeted walkway onto an elaborate stage on the fifty-yard line to accept his party's presidential nomination.

Following the speech, movie sound track style music blared out through hundreds of speakers and rockets shot into the air from tall columns placed on either side of the stage as the newly minted candidates, Barack Obama and Joe Biden, moved downstage to bathe in the adoration of the stadium crowd. To be fair, it was a significant moment in American history. After hundreds of years of slavery and racial oppression, Barack Obama was the first African-American nominated for president by a major political party. All the same, the coverage of the event by the media, facilitated by a squad of *logos*-knowing planners, was loud and clear: 70,000 people can't be wrong. It was the principle of social proof played out on a grand scale, the supreme wisdom of the crowd.[27]

Which, in a strange roundabout way, brings us back to organized religion in this age of *mythos* knowing. The pastor who gave the invocation at President Obama's inauguration in 2009 was Rick Warren of Saddleback Valley Community Church in Orange County, California. While many mainline Protestant and Catholic pastors have watched as their congregations gray, their pews empty, and their positions as spiritual guides and respected community leaders are undermined by the new electronic mythmakers, Saddleback Valley Community Church is doing just fine. One of a new breed of mega-churches sprouting up in communities across the country, many in well-to-do suburbs of large cities, Saddleback has seen its attendance numbers grow by leaps and bounds. Founded in 1996 with fewer than two hundred members, the church now hosts more that twenty-two thousand "seekers" each weekend at its main campus, as well as another five thousand at its four satellite campuses.

Saddleback is by no means the largest mega-church in America. According to Forbes Magazine, The Second Baptist Church of Houston accommodates nearly 24,000 visitors each weekend spread out across five campuses and has an annual operating budget of fifty-three million dollars—a "town within a city" as its pastor, Edwin Young, describes his church.

Lakewood Church, the home church of pastor and best-selling author Joel Osteen, is the largest mega-church in the nation. Also located in Houston, Lakewood paid the city $13 million for a sixty-year lease on the Compaq Center, former home of the Houston Rockets. The church then invested an

---

27. To add an element of mythos-knowing resonance, candidate Obama gave his speech on the forty-fifth anniversary of the famous "I Have A Dream" speech by Martin Luther King.

additional $95 million renovating the 650,000-square-foot building, which included installing wall-to-wall carpeting and cushioned theater-style seating for 14,000 people. They also installed three enormous video screens, the largest thirty-two feet by eighteen feet, upon which the congregation can watch the media-friendly faces of Pastor Joel and his wife Victoria preach their sermons. Perhaps most impressive structural feature is the stage with a revolving golden globe of the earth in the center and waterfalls on either end that can be programmed so the flow of water crescendos at peak moments during the worship service.[28]

Mega-churches, defined as Protestant congregations of 2,000 or more, are the descendants and rightful heirs of the *mythos*-knowing tent revival of yore. In 1970, there were 50 mega-churches in the United States; today that number has grown to more than 1,300. They offer state-of-the-art sound and lighting systems, fitness centers, food courts, Internet cafes, information desks, bookstores, special VIP seating, armies of greeters, and performances by Christian rock bands and other nationally known celebrities. Many have television and radio broadcast facilities and employ their own security personnel— Lakewood Church has a twelve-officer police force. They also have extensive childcare facilities. Lakewood calls their childcare center "Kidspace," which is described on the church's web site as, "A place where kids can have a great big life with a great big God. A place where loving God is cool and kids rule!" Lakewood is clearly comfortable with the concept of BIG. An

---

28. Like Ted Turner, Joel Osteen's first career was in the media business where he built KTBU-TV55 into a successful independent television station for the Houston market. He took over Lakewood Church after his father, John Osteen, the founding pastor, died in 1999.

innovator in the pastoral marketplace, Lakewood offers a drive-through healing service conducted by Rev. Osteen's mother-in-law.

According to Forbes, mega-churches and their celebrity pastors generate income in excess of $8.5 billion dollars per year. It is understandable, then, that many of the evangelical mega-churches learned to exploit a fruitful marriage between *mythos* and *logos* knowing. Many of the top leaders are highly trained professionals, as familiar with the theories of mezzanine financing, debt/equity ratios, and backflush costing as they are with the texts of the New Testament. The senior pastor of Carson Valley Christian Centre in Nevada, for instance, refers to himself as a "PastorPrenuer." He has even published a book by that title. The Willow Creek Community Church employs two MBAs, one from Harvard and another from Stanford.

Like the film and music industry and broadcast and cable television networks who employ serious numbers of MBAs and market researchers, the mega-churches' appeal and interface with the people in the seats out front is straight-ahead *mythos* knowing, as was the case with the Christian Church of Europe during the Middle Ages.

Or to quote King Solomon, "What has been, will be again. What has been done, will be done again. There is nothing new under the sun."

My mother taught me when I was young that it is rude to discuss politics, religion, or a woman's age in polite company. Well, leaving a woman's age aside, I believe we must discuss politics and religion if we are to understand how they are currently orchestrated by *mythos*-knowing mediums and *logos*-knowing organizational practices. The first time McCain and Obama met to debate during their 2008 campaign, they met at Rick Warren's Saddleback Valley Community Church with Pastor

Warren serving as the moderator. The victor in that election, Barack Obama, later invited Dr. Warren to give the invocation at his inauguration.

But are the mega-churches successful because of their content? In other words, do they preach a better gospel, a more relevant message for our times? It is hard to say, but if we consider the mega-church as a medium, it becomes apparent that they owe much of their spectacular growth to their appreciation for and willingness to adopt the communication mediums of the electronic age.

A growing trend among mega-churches is the practice of renting commercial multiplex movie theaters for Sunday morning worship services. This gives the church an opportunity to offer themed services tailored to a variety of demographic groups. Thus in one theater you'll find a service for young families featuring lots of upbeat contemporary music, while in an adjoining theater the service is geared to the country-western crowd. A traditional service is held in yet another theater for older members. The sermon for each, however, remains the same because it is electronically piped in from the mother church and digitally projected onto the theater screens featuring the charismatic storytelling preacher who made the mega-church so successful to begin with.

In 2009, National CineMedia, which is jointly owned by movie theater chains AMC, Regal, and Cinemark, managed rentals for 1,400 churches nationwide, as compared to six years ago when they managed only three church rentals, an astounding increase of 1,397 churches who are using movie theaters for worship services in just six years.

Mark Batterson, lead pastor of National Community Church, which rents movie theaters in the Washington, D.C. area and hosts an annual conference for theater churches says, "Movie screens are postmodern stained glass. We're using moving pictures to tell the gospel to a post-literate culture. There are ways of doing church that no one has thought of yet. We have to live with the tension of being biblically true and culturally relevant."

Pastor Mark sees the ascendancy of the *mythos* knowing in the modern world and knows it is time to climb on board. Willow Creek Community Church began in a movie theater in 1975 with only 125 attendees. The church now has its own worship center where over 20,000 attend each weekend.

Pastor Wes Beavis of Destiny People Christian Church in Irvine, California, holds services in movies theaters as well. He was quoted in the *Los Angeles Times* saying, "We'd be lost without the screen. The great thing about it is that it's huge. We fill it with my messages, PowerPoint presentations, words to songs, and great images of nature."

Sometimes Pastor Wes shows a scene from a mainstream Hollywood film like *The Legend of Bagger Vance* starring Will Smith and Matt Damon, about a disillusioned man who takes up golf. He wanted to tell a story about the importance of determination and so he showed the film on the big screen at the Stadium 10 Cinemas in Irvine's Market Place mall as part of the worship service.

Barry Brown is the director of Worship Solutions with the CineMedia Company, and he talked to me about the appeal of turning movie theaters into temporary churches.

"People are using the technology as a driver or as a mechanism to get a message from point A to point B more quickly via video, versus live in person. But I think the venue also has a big thing to do with the rapid rise in theater church growth. From a social standpoint, we're conditioned to go into a movie theater and be quiet and see something on the screen. That is a driver from an emotional perspective, whether it's a comedy, drama or horror movie, we're conditioned to hear a story. So naturally we're already programmed walking through the theater door to receive a story, and your interpretation of the story may be different than if it was in a different venue because you weren't conditioned that way when you walked in the door, whether it is in a school, or a church building, or a storefront of another location. Cognitively speaking, when you walked into the theater, you walked in to hear a story."

Mr. Brown talked about taking God's word into the marketplace, into the shopping malls that are America's new main streets. He said that initially some church pastors complained about the Hollywood film posters in the lobbies, many of which they considered profane and sinful. But since the posters cannot be taken down, they have come to accept them as part of the troubled secular world they are striving to transform. According to Mr. Brown, it is part of the ephemeral nature of these new churches. He sees it as an advantage.

"Well, it's a portable church, right? From our pastors' standpoint, while they aren't physically building a building, they're building a church, they're setting up equipment, they're tearing down equipment, they're setting up the children's ministry, they're setting up welcome centers and things like that. They're also setting up audiovisual equipment. So they're setting up a worship sanctuary, for lack of a better term, each and every week, which lends itself, from the standpoint of churchgoers, being able to get plugged in more quickly than they would in a traditional facility, because there are more volunteer opportunities in a *portable* environment than there is in a traditional church facility. I think the unchurched and the dechurched are more willing to check it out because they feel like there is not as much stigma attached to it, because it isn't a physical church building. It's something new and different from whatever their preconceived notion of church has been." [29]

29. Listening to Mr. Brown, I found myself thinking about Ireland in the

* * *

A few years ago a question concerning the siting of cell towers in England threw the Christian religious community into a quandary that pitted the traditional role of churches against the emerging *mythos*-knowing technologies of today. Cell phone use around the world is expanding exponentially, but this matters little to some English homeowner associations who are determined to keep cell towers out of their communities. They claim the towers are both eyesores and possible sources of carcinogenic radiation. On the other hand, practically everyone in the world is queuing up to buy the handy little devices, which won't work without the towers—a situation to delight any gorgon.

Enter the churches of England, those majestic ivy-blanketed stone structures that hearken back to when God was in His Heaven and Britannia ruled the seas. Nearly every cobblestone village and hamlet in England has a church, its tall steep spire reaching up above the bucolic landscape, the very landscape the anti-cell tower crowd was determined to protect. But many of these same churches were also broke; decreased church attendance in this secular age meant less cash to pay for gutter replacements, electric service upgrades, and fuel oil to keep the drafty old churches warm through the winter.

Then someone came up with a great *logos*-knowing idea, a true marriage of convenience: why not hide cell masts

---

17th and 18th centuries, when English Protestants outlawed celebrating mass. Priests would travel incognito through the countryside, their altar a rough-hewn board laid across two barrels inside a barn, or a large flat stone in a field under the stars. A number of these priests saying mass with their backs to the congregants were shot and killed by British agents. These crude altars are called mass stones. I suspect this period of persecution did more to wed the Irish to Catholicism than all the impressive architectural and ecclesiastical frills of Trinity Cathedral.

inside the steeples of the old churches? Most steeples are tall enough and the tower would be completely hidden from view. What people cannot see, will not bother them. Besides, the telecommunications industry has oodles of money, and the churches need a new source of income—bingo!

So telecom companies began offering churches as much as $20,000 to rent their steeples for a year, and village vicars across England drew a collective sigh of relief. But then a small but earnest congregation in Chingford in northeast London objected to the potential health risks from having a cell tower in the steeple of their church. The church leadership responded by bringing in a cadre of *logos*-knowing experts to refute the claims, so the protesters switched over to a *mythos*-knowing argument: since more and more information is being sent and received on cell phones, and since some of that information is pornographic and/or obscene, then the church must refuse to be a party to such transmissions.[30]

The church hierarchy then entered the fray on the pro-cell tower side, asserting that any "ill" posed by the towers was outweighed by the "benefits." They pointed out that even Guildford Cathedral had a cell mast hidden just beneath its golden angel weather vane.

But the protesters were undeterred, and they filed a suit with the diocesan judge who ruled in their favor, agreeing that "revolting and damaging" pornography could be transmitted by the network.

The church in Chingford appealed to the Archbishop of Canterbury's 800-year-old Court of Arches. This august body overturned the lower court's ruling, permitting the installation; but, alas, all this took several years, and, in the meantime, the

---

30. May I suggest here a minor revision of the version of Lord's prayer I learned in my youth, to wit: "and forgive us our transmissions as we forgive those who transmit against us."

telecom company had gone out of business and another had installed a tower in the car park across the street from the church.

An addendum to this story: in the mid-1970s, I lived for a year in the hills above Inverness, Scotland. I was there to study the traditional fiddle music of the Highlands but I also took a class in bell ringing at the local cathedral. We met one evening a week and climbed a steep narrow wooden stairway into the bell tower where we pulled long ropes to start the bells ringing. I still remember the feel of the heavy rope in my hands and the pleasant and oddly comforting vibration the tolling bells produce inside my body. But since you must pay careful attention to the laws of momentum, bell ringing has its *logos* side also: too little force and the great bells remain mute, too much and you risk snapping the wooden stop that prevents the bell from swinging all the way over and possibly breaking loose. Years later, while researching the cell tower controversy in England, I came across a newspaper article about a group of bell ringers refusing to perform their task because they were worried about radiation exposure from the cell tower inside the steeple of their church. I see a certain irony in this: in an effort to maintain the visual purity of the English countryside, cell towers were installed in church steeples, allowing ring tones of every variety to sound for miles around inside purses and jacket pockets, on dressers and the dashboards of cars, all the while causing the ancient, proud bells to go silent.

We finish this section on technology and religious storytelling with an observation from the world of televangelism. It takes considerable skill to enchant an audience. It also takes humor. I remember the first time I came across a broadcast of John Hagee giving a sermon. One second he was talking to his flock about Moses and the next he was telling a joke, which went something like this:

A farmer was on his way to town one day when he passed a farmhouse. The people who lived in the house invited the farmer inside because they wanted to show him a jigsaw puzzle they'd just completed. The puzzle made the picture of an old stone mill with a waterwheel and deer standing in a nearby meadow.

"That's right pretty," the farmer said to the beaming family. "How long did it take you to put together?"

"Six months," the father said while his wife and kids nodded their heads. "We all worked on it, day and night. There are two hundred and fifty pieces in that puzzle."

"Six months?" the farmer said scratching his jaw, "But ain't that an awfully long time to put a puzzle together?"

"Why no," said the mother. "It says right here on the box: 'Seven to ten years.'"

This practice of using humor to get a more serious message across is as old as the hills. A storyteller must first "jolly up the audience," as the Rev. Gantry would say, in order to draw them into the tent to sell them the goods, be the goods patent medicine, a set of Ginsu knives, or eternal salvation. Again, we are considering *how* it is done, the use of the medium, and not whether one brand of medicine or spiritual salvation is any better or truer than another.

As for Reverend Hagee, he is a self-described Pentecostal hellfire-and-brimstone preacher who pastors a large church in San Antonio, Texas. The Trinity Broadcast Network airs his sermons across the nation so that they are included in the basic cable package offered by most cable television companies. Hagee also writes best-selling books with uplifting titles like *From Daniel to Doomsday*, *Jerusalem Countdown*, and his latest *Can America Survive? 10 Prophetic Signs That We Are the Terminal*

Generation, which—you will be happy to learn—are available online at www.armageddon.com. The last time I visited my local Barnes and Noble I also found a entire sales table devoted exclusively to Reverend Hagee's books, which, it's accurate to say, are meant to scare the hell out of you.

As we saw, it was John McCain's association with John Hagee that landed him in hot water with the powerful conservative Catholics of his party. Hagee has since apologized for his denigrating remarks about Catholics, and yet the Texas preacher still believes that the United States should preemptively attack Iran, that Hurricane Katrina was God's way of punishing a sinful New Orleans, that Russia will invade Israel, and that the president of the European Union will become the Antichrist. In other words, John Hagee buys into that old *mythos*-knowing tribalism in a big way.

I recently watched another preacher run a televised TBN fundraiser to pay for a new communication satellite to assure that, "the gospel of Christ can be preached to every part of the world." He explained that this effort to place satellites in orbit constituted one of the "signs" of the End Times as prophesied in the Book of Revelations. He then read the relevant passage as a photograph of a satellite appeared on the screen, a bright long silver cylinder suspended against the blackness of space with a pair of solar panels extending out from each side like the wings of an angel.

"And I saw an angel flying in mid-heaven, having an eternal Good News to proclaim to those who dwell on the earth, and to every nation, tribe, language, and people. He said with a loud voice, 'Fear the Lord, and give him glory; for the hour of his judgment has come. Worship him who made the heaven, the earth, the sea, and the springs of waters!'"

Now, you have to admit, that is as creative a blending of theology and technology as you could wish for.

CHAPTER 15

Four Corners

I HAVE A WRITING OFFICE UPSTAIRS in the First Christian Church in downtown Olympia, Washington. First Christian is a Disciples of Christ church, a liberal-minded Protestant denomination organized in Olympia in 1891, and even though I am not an official member, they graciously let me write my books in their spare room. The church also serves as an overnight shelter for homeless families with children. They provide space for Alcoholics Anonymous meetings, a debtors' counseling group, and miscellaneous groups who are doing good work in the community.

The congregation is mostly elderly, and they recently hired a newly ordained pastor in the hopes she can attract younger people and families to join the current congregation or perhaps start another congregation somewhere away from downtown Olympia.

Well, one day last winter I decided to take a stroll and catch some sunshine and, as I stepped out of the church at the corner of 7th and Franklin, I was suddenly struck by how the buildings on this corner represent a sort of microcosm of what I had been trying to put on paper, the relationship and tensions between the institutions of *mythos*-knowing and *logos*-knowing in the world today.

Kitty-corner across the intersection from First Christian is the former Carnegie Library, which was vacated in 1978 when the new library was built a block away. A software development company occupied the building for several years, but it has been recently taken over by The Reality Church, one of the many new technologically-savvy churches that, although not a mega-church, incorporate cutting edge communication devices to attract and engage their members. Their logo is a black and white silhouette of a hand, thumb and fingers extended, with a small circle near the center of the palm suggestive of an eye or a nail hole. This sigil is painted on a large sign on the lawn in front and is silk-screened onto the awning leading up the steps to the front door. On the sign under the logo are the words, "Following Christ, Serving Our Community."

Inside the open-floor plan of The Reality Church, a stage equipped with professional-grade lighting and a sound system takes the place of the traditional chancel with altar and pulpit. The worship service includes a sermon with the minister speaking into a wireless microphone as he roams freely back and forth across the stage. There is a great deal of spirited singing led by a rock band with drums and electric guitars. Facing the stage are rows of red upholstered seats with cup holders in the armrests that were purchased from a movie theater. On the other end of this large room is a gourmet coffee bar with a sitting area of cozy stuffed chairs and couches where church members and visitors can hang out and savor a freshly brewed cappuccino.

The young and enthusiastic pastor, Paul Jones, comes from a long line of fundamentalist preachers on both sides of his family. While in college pursuing a degree in history with the goal of becoming a high school history teacher, he attended an outdoor music festival in Oregon and felt God speak to him. That was the moment he decided to become a minister.

So you have these two churches facing each other diagonally across the intersection. The older, First Christian, is a church where *logos* knowing is highly valued. Across the hallway from the sanctuary, with its vaulted ceiling and stained glass, there is a spacious library where book groups meet to discuss ideas such as morality in modern society. Most, if not all, the members embrace the theory of evolution and a woman's right to choose. Members of the Queer community are likewise accepted as part of God's family. So while the medium, the physical structure of the church, is old-fashioned by today's *mythos*-knowing standards, the content of its cultural and political views is quite modern.

By comparison, The Reality Church, as a medium exudes an aura of being contemporary and relevant. To aid the singers, for example, song lyrics are projected on a large screen above the stage in place of printed hymnals, such as those used at First Christian.

When it comes to their message, however, The Reality Church is surprisingly traditional. They are strictly opposed to abortion, although they do not picket abortion clinics. They also consider homosexuality a sin—the pastor refers to it as "broken" sexuality. As people of the "Word," they adopt a literal interpretation of the Bible obeying what they see as the laws of God as revealed through the prophets of the Old Testament while following the teachings of Jesus and his disciples, including Paul of Tarsus and John of Patmos, author of the Book of Revelations.

Entering The Reality Church can be slightly confusing given that the words CARNEGIE LIBRARY remain carved into the stone lintel above the front door, mute testimony to the fact that the building was once among those cherished temples of *logos* knowing found in so many towns big and small across America.

Meanwhile, a combination printing business and copy shop occupies the southeast corner of the intersection at 7th and Franklin, a humble *logos*-knowing descendent of Johann Gutenberg. The shop is a secular space where, since 1974, citizens of Olympia have come to get their business forms and merchant discount coupon books printed and their real estate flyers, term papers, and resumes copied at six cents a page, the best rates in town. Interestingly, the owners, citing both financial and psychological reasons, refuse to print wedding invitations and funeral programs, those harbingers of the most *mythos*-knowing rituals in our society.

On the remaining corner of the intersection is the Washington State Office of the Superintendent of Public Instruction, housed in the former state house, an elegantly expansive cut-stone building with great arched entranceways and spires reaching to the sky—and on the lawn a life-sized bronze statue of General Washington kneeling in prayer. OSPI is an organization that struggles daily with the conflict between *mythos* and *logos* knowing. With unacceptably high dropout rates, pervasive drug and alcohol use among young people, gang-related violence, and a variety of other tough social problems impacting schools, the state public education system finds its traditional role of fostering *logos* knowing being increasingly undermined by the influence of the entertainment industry and popular culture.[31]

31. Like other states in recent years, Washington has turned to standardized testing as a way to shore up its *logos*-knowing mission. Meanwhile, teachers and school administrators in Atlanta and other public school districts around the country have confessed to systematically altering standardized test scores for hundreds of students in order to meet benchmarks set for student achievement by the No Child Left Behind legislation. With university schools of education, textbook publishers, test preparation companies, software developers, think tanks, and educational consultants on one side and a pervasive electronic entertainment industry, including radio, television, film, computer gaming, and

Countless times I have heard educators bemoan the fact that they must compete every day with movie actors, rock stars, and television personalities for the attention, respect, cooperation, and affection of young people. Teachers realize they cannot be as exciting or glamorous as Ben Affleck or Natalie Portman and that their classrooms, outfitted with tired desks, buzzing fluorescent lights, and scuffed linoleum floors, are poor cousins to the multiplex movie theaters with their plush seats, carpeted walkways, and velvet-draped screens. Young people observe these differences and correctly interpret them to mean that we as a society value the world of electronic entertainment far above the world of public education.

Compare for a moment the working realities of a typical public school teacher with a film star like Cameron Diaz who plays a foul-mouthed middle school teacher in the film *Bad Teacher* opposite fellow star Justin Timberlake. Our typical teacher, we'll call her Sandra, wakes up in the morning to her clock radio, takes a quick shower, and then brews a cup of coffee. She pops a bagel in the toaster and grabs a yogurt from the refrigerator. If she has children, she packs them a lunch for school, makes sure their clothes are clean, and signs their homework packets. After sending them out the door, she hits the freeway in her Honda Civic to battle rush-hour traffic. Once in her classroom, she has a short time to collect her thoughts and arrange the day's lessons before the bell rings and her students arrive. She spends the day teaching, admonishing, mediating conflicts, entering grades, administering state-mandated tests, attending staff meetings, monitoring the playground or cafeteria, collecting and assigning homework, examining Billy for lice and sending him to the office, helping students prepare for the upcoming science/history/medieval fair, conducting

---

Internet social networks on the other, educators find themselves at the flash point where the interests of *logos* and *mythos* knowing vie for dominance.

parent/teacher conferences, and perhaps spending an extra hour or two coaching volleyball or soccer. She then drives herself home, stopping at the supermarket to buy groceries. After cooking dinner, she corrects more student papers before catching a few minutes of television and going to bed.

Ms. Diaz, meanwhile, is awakened by a call from her service, and while her private chef serves her a nutritious meal of poached salmon and elderberry pancakes, a maid makes her bed and straightens her room. Then Ms. Diaz's personal trainer/ yoga instructor leads her through a quick morning workout, after which she showers before climbing into a chauffeur-driven stretch limo that whisks her to the movie studio or a location shoot. Inside her personal trailer, a stylist does her hair while a make-up artist brushes her delicate cheeks with rouge, or perhaps dabs on a mite more foundation to cover an ornery pimple. The costumer arrives with her outfit and helps her dress while a script assistant helps her rehearse her lines—depending on the part she is to play that day, she might also receive the services of a speech/dialect coach. She steps onto the set and waits as technicians carefully adjust the lighting to make her look her very best; the cameraman might employ a filter to give her skin a bit more radiance or to hide worry lines. An experienced director gives her last minute instructions before she performs a scene made up of a series of short takes, none longer than a few minutes in length. The rest of the time she sits and waits, a bottle of sparkling French mineral water in her hand as the stylist combs a rogue strand of hair back into place. It is all a bit tedious, really, but light years away from Sandra who is trying to help a handful of confused, hormone-laced young people find their way in the world.

As for the rest of Ms. Diaz's day, there's the gala awards event, an appearance on *The Tonight Show*, or dinner with her agent at a swanky LA restaurant. In addition to her agent, she a publicist, lawyer, and personal manager to promote and protect her interests, as well as a pool boy, gardener, tennis pro—well, you get the idea. We value our Diazs and Timberlakes, our *mythos*-knowing actors and their well-paid directors and producers, while those engaged in the demanding *logos*-knowing work of educating our children for the future are lucky, given recent budget cuts, if they can keep their jobs for another year, all the while hoping to avoid being disciplined for failing to improve test scores, sued for some form of harassment, or castigated by a parent or minister for reading or telling an inappropriate folktale.

This last instance happened occasionally to my wife Paula and me when schools hired us to tell stories and play music. At first I was taken aback by these attacks since the stories I told, a wizard turning a nosey woman into a woodpecker, for instance, or Uncle Jay trying to save his sick wife by gathering up Death in a burlap sack and sticking him in a hollowed out apple tree, were considerably tamer than most of the supernatural stories coming out the entertainment industry today. Besides, in the old tales good always defeats evil, and usually through cleverness and virtue rather than through violence. So what were the parents and ministers complaining about? Then it came to me: they were concerned, perhaps legitimately so, about the debasing influence that television and film violence, sex, and vulgarity was having on their children but frustrated because they had no access to the heads of Viacom, Paramount, or even Disney. They could, however, complain to their local school principal or a school board member about the visiting storyteller. And even though only a very small number of individuals complained, the principal would get nervous and ask me to talk to the parents. In nearly every case they withdrew their protest after I told them the offending story. It was a funny dance, really, and I often felt I was being cast in the role of surrogate for an industry that keeps itself successfully walled off from the concerns of ordinary citizens.

We can appreciate how highly we value *mythos* knowing in our society today by comparing the amount of money we pay individuals to perform certain jobs. Looking at predominately *logos*-knowing occupations, we find that a district judge here in Washington State makes $134,233 a year. A United State Supreme Court judge such as Justice Sonia Sotomayor earns a salary of $213,900 a year. By comparison, television's "Judge Judy" Sheindlin is paid $45 million a year. The national average salary for a family physician is between $117,000 and $159,000 a year. The actor Hugh Laurie who plays a physician on the television show *House M.D.* is paid $400,000 a year. The national average salary for a police detective is between $46,000 and $81,000. Actors Christopher Meloni and Mariska Hargitay who costar on *Law and Order: Special Victims Unit* are each paid $395,000 a year. Lastly, the veteran actor Martin Sheen, who played the fictional president Josiah Bartlett for seven years on *The West Wing* received $300,000 an episode, for a yearly salary of $6,600,000. That is sixteen times more than what the real President of the United States earns in a year.

Of course, the *logos*-knowing CEOs of a number of multinational corporations continue to do quite well in the money department, although they increasingly find they must hone their *mythos*-knowing skills to survive. As with General Stanley McChrystal, it was Tony Hayward's failure to deal successfully with the media—an unguarded remark about wanting his life back, not the oil spill itself—that cost him his job as the head of BP. But when it comes to public service, the discrepancies between the financial compensation given to *logos*-trained and *mythos*-trained individuals are most extreme. While Cameron Diaz earns between $10 and $20 million per film, the average salary for a middle school teacher in the United States in 2012 is $42,460.

Another window into the kinds of popular cultural forces school teachers and administrators are up against can be found in the phenomena of Harry Potter, without question one of the most successful franchises in the history of mass media. J.K. Rowling's books tell the story of an abused orphan who one day discovers that he is a wizard and is whisked off to wizard school by an affable giant named Hagrid. Suffice it to say, it is nearly impossible to live in the United States in the twenty-first century, or elsewhere for that matter, and not know about Harry Potter and his cohorts Ron and Hermione, who have become heroes to a generation of children and to many of their parents.

Each book in the seven volume series has been a monster bestseller, and, because books tend to promote reading, Harry Potter is lauded as a positive force supporting *logos* knowing. Organizations such as the American Library Association have honored Ms. Rowling's efforts with awards, and yet, if we consider the films that have been made from the novels, we may conclude that this assessment is not entirely accurate. These lavish cinematic confections feature a who's who list of the most respected actors on the planet including Maggie Smith, Michael Gambon, Kenneth Branagh, John Hurt, Emma Watson, Ralph Fiennes, Miranda Richardson, Gary Oldman, Jim Broadbent, Richard Harris, and Helena Bonham Carter. The films are robust delights for the senses for which no expense was spared. What kid in his or her right mind would not choose Hogwarts School of Witchcraft and Wizardry over the underfunded and dingy public high school down the street? Hogwarts is without doubt the best *mythos*-knowing school imaginable, a place crammed full of marvel and surprise.

At Hogwarts, students learn by doing. They mix magic potions, cavort with rare mythological creatures, and recite incantations that produce immediate results, even if the results are only half-right, such as when Ron tries to turn his pet rat into a glass goblet. Professor McGonagall has already demonstrated for the class how it's done, effortlessly transforming a macaw into a goblet with the slight touch of her magic wand. Only Ron's rat becomes a furry cup with a long tail, providing his desk partner, Harry, a moment of affectionate hilarity.

And that is how school is presented throughout the first four Harry Potter films. But in the fifth, *Harry Potter and the Order of the Phoenix*, the agents of *logos* knowing invade the hallowed halls of Hogwarts to ruin all the fun. The chief villain, the Snidely Whiplash of this melodrama, is Delores Umbridge, who is assigned by the bureaucrats at the Ministry of Magic to teach the Defense Against the Dark Arts class, and who later replaces the beloved Albus Dumbledore as headmistress of Hogwarts. She is the stereotypical uptight, rule-bound, emotionally stunted, irritatingly singsong, *logos*-knowing schoolmarm. In a pivotal scene, she addresses the students while standing in front of an enormous slow swinging pendulum, reinforcing her connection to *logos* knowing as it holds to the constraints of sequential time. She informs her young charges that henceforth all lessons will be learned, not from practical, real world sensual experiences, but from textbooks. Harry and his companion wizards and witches-in-training handle these textbooks as if they are incomprehensible slabs of stone. They complain. They argue. They whine. But Ms. Umbridge, beaming her infuriating know-it-all smile, stands her ground, refusing budge, gleefully explaining that they have to prepare for their OWLs, a series of standardized tests that will be administered to gauge their progress as students.

The scene then cuts to a long, gloomy study hall filled with desks set in rows like letters on a page, where students wrestle with sheaves of test papers. There is no talking, no laughing, no magical turning birds or rats into cups. It is time for drudgery, the old nose-to-the-grindstone style of *logos* knowing. Scratch, scratch, scratch—the students struggle to fill in the correct answers on the test forms, Ron rubbing his head in frustration, Harry looking up now and again to glare at Ms. Umbridge with unconcealed loathing. He knows these tedious paper-and-pen drills will not protect them from Lord Voldemort, the dreaded dark wizard who is out to take over Hogwarts and kill Harry. What the students need are real experiences, not a bunch of book learning.

But precisely when there seems to be no escape from the stultifying test, the rambunctious, mutinous Weasley twins swoop into the test room on their broomsticks, sucking the test papers into the air in their back draft and setting off cascades of iridescent fireworks. The students cheer as Ms. Umbridge and the cranky old janitor Argus Filch look on with anxious bewilderment. What is happening to their beloved *logos* knowing? How can they regain control? Alas, it is too late. The students quit their desks and run after the Weasley twins as they zoom out of the hall and a distressed and disheveled Ms. Umbridge stumbles after them. But as she passes under the doorway the hundred or more heavy plaques hanging on the wall upon which she has posted her rules begin falling and crashing down all around her, so that she must cover her head to keep from getting clobbered.

The students, however, are ecstatic as Fred and George fly off into the bright, sunlit sky, having thoroughly demolished *logos* knowing and restored *mythos* knowing to its rightful place. Even Professor Filius Flitwick, the diminutive part-goblin charms master, after a quick glance over his shoulder to make sure none of the adults are watching, gives a victorious fist pump in solidarity with the cheerful and liberated students.

When I talk to high school students, this is the part of my presentation that "really grabs 'em," again as Reverend Gantry would say. Most have seen the Harry Potter movies and maybe they sense what this particular scene is saying, "Don't trust that dry old *logos* knowing, the endless reading, analysis, fact checking, and more fact checking. Instead, trust your gut, rely on your senses, your intuition, throw yourself into the physical realities of this marvelous world and discover what you're made of, that is the only way to learn."

Or as the disembodied voice of Ben "Obi-Wan" Kenobi advises Luke Skywalker as the young man pilots his X-fighter toward the Death Star in the Star Wars film, "Use the force, Luke. Let go."

And Luke does. He switches off the *logos*-knowing technology, the sophisticated computer fire-control system, and relying instead on *mythos* knowing to guide his actions, he is able to destroy the Empire's greatest weapon, the very essence of machine-ruled *logos*-knowing culture.

What is important to keep in mind when considering films like *Harry Potter and the Order of the Phoenix* or *Star Wars* is the agenda of the entity that produced it. What stake did the storyteller have, Heyday Films in the case of Harry Potter, in the increasingly rancorous and personal contest between *mythos* and *logos* knowing? Are they disinterested parties or do they have a dog in the fight?

On the whole, electronic *mythos*-knowing media companies want young people, and the rest of us as well, to look to them for "truth," instead of looking to the traditional *logos*-knowing institutions of schools, print journalism, science, and the judicial system.

This is not surprising given that film studios and television production companies draw their wealth and cultural clout from *mythos* knowing. Why not craft stories that celebrate *mythos* knowing, the kind of stories that encourage people to make critical political decisions, the kind of decisions upon which their survival and that of their children depend, by using their instincts? Instead of judging a candidate based on his or her experience, voting record, or on what corporation is funding the campaign, *mythos* knowing focuses on the candidate's affect. Is he tall and does he have all his hair? Is he real man or a wimp? Is she alluring and strong or just another whining manhater? It follows that more attention was given by some of the cable news programs and radio talk shows during the 2008 presidential campaign to how much cuter Sarah Palin was than Nancy Pelosi, rather than on how well either of them govern.

National Public Radio likes to talk about "driveway moments," when a story is so interesting you wait in your car until it ends. A friend of mine had a unique *mythos*-knowing driveway moment during the 2008 election campaign. He was in the car with his six-year-old daughter and they were listening to Barack Obama give a speech on the radio. As they pulled up to the house, he switched off the radio and was about to open the door when his daughter said, "Leave it on Daddy, I like hearing the man *sing*."

If you like how a candidate dresses and combs her hair, the timbre of his voice and how he gets angry—"I paid for this microphone," —or how he moves—"some folks look at me and see swagger, which in Texas is called 'walking,'"—then you'll most likely warm to her ideas even though they run contrary to your own self-interest.

The human brain is wired to learn through what I call the "trinity of durable learning:" emotion, association, and action. When an event or person triggers emotion inside us, adrenaline is secreted in the brain, which fixes memory. That is why effective advertising relies heavily on evocative images and sounds to stir up our emotions. The adrenaline released during the initial experience chemically welds the memory into our brains, which also explains why traumatic events can have such a lasting impact on the mind's psychological health.

The second element necessary for long-term learning is association, the way the brain links new information or experience to something it already knows.

A simple experiment:

Say the word "post" three times out loud.

Post. Post. Post.

Now, what do you put in a toaster?

If you said "bread," give yourself a star. But if you said "toast," then you experienced how association works inside the brain.

It is much easier to carve a piece of wood like maple or ash by going *with* the grain of the wood rather than *against* it. The same is true for the brain. It has its own grain, an inherent tendency to relate one piece of information to another. That is why for many years the magazine with the most dollar-for-dollar tobacco advertising was not *Cosmopolitan*, *Esquire*, or even *Playboy*. It was *Sports Illustrated*, because the marketing geniuses at R. J. Reynolds and Philip Morris knew that by associating their products with healthy activities like baseball, tennis, and skiing, people would forget about the dire health risks they were taking. The *mythos*-knowing part of the brain in particular would fail to make the distinction. The same holds true for McDonald's decision to host the 2012 Summer Olympics.

The third component of durable learning is putting the lesson learned into action. This internalizes the lesson, making it a part of us. Going back to tobacco advertising, the brands that ran the most aggressive coupon programs—the ones where customers sent in coupons from packs of cigarettes for ball caps, backpacks, and stadium blankets—were Marlboro and Camel, the most popular brands with teenagers. The tobacco companies did not care if they lost money on the transaction. What they knew from their research was that the simple act of filling in the coupon and mailing it would significantly strengthen a customer's loyalty to their brand. When it came to a newly addicted young person that meant a highly profitable lifetime relationship with the "consumer."

The same thing happens in school when a teacher teaching a scientific theory provides students with an opportunity to apply the theory in the real world. I made a functioning volcano in fifth grade using chicken wire and plaster of paris for the mountain and vinegar and baking soda for the eruption. Watching the lava bubbling out of the top was exciting—that was the emotion—I knew my mother and grandmother cooked using vinegar and baking soda, that was the association—and I was given the chance to put it all together and watch it happen, the action. Add a dash more emotion because I was very fond of Sister Cornelia, my fifth grade teacher, and I still have that memory and the knowledge, even though most of the learning experiences I had that year in fifth grade I could not recall if my life depended on it.

Selling cigarettes and candidates are actually very similar enterprises. People respond to a series of carefully crafted, highly charged television ads, positive or negative; it does not matter so long as they are packed with emotion and compelling associations: candidate Smith will stop the spread of socialism, candidate Lopez will save Medicare, candidate Hogan will keep criminals off the streets, candidate Russo will show that guy in Iran who's boss.

Lastly, the people are encouraged to act: to donate money, attend rallies, canvas their neighborhood, and put up campaign posters. And when election day rolls around, they are encouraged to pull a lever, tap a touch screen, or mail in a ballot, and so internalize—we could say tribalize—their relationship with the candidate and the party. It is a hard combination to resist, especially when served up by the kind of behavioral experts and media creatives who work for political campaigns.

And if there is a fourth cylinder to this peppy emotion, association, and action engine it is repetition. Do or say something enough times and it sticks in the mind as true. Sarah Palin, for instance, repeatedly attacked Obama's health care plan by claiming that the government was going to set up "death panels." This was false, but those who through emotion, association, and action identified with Palin, naturally believed it was true. Run enough television ads showing verdant rural landscapes dotted with pristine lakes, children with happy faces boarding yellow school buses, and impeccably maintained high-tech drilling equipment, and people will believe that hydraulic fracking for natural gas does not, in fact, pollute ground water or contribute to global warming, or for that matter, that rising CO_2 levels in the atmosphere poses any real threat to our survival.

CHAPTER 16

A Question of Leadership

I ONCE GAVE A SPEECH ABOUT THE INFLUENCE of modern media on young people at a juvenile justice conference in Reno, Nevada. My wife and I were staying at the conference hotel, and one evening we went to the pool area to soak in the Jacuzzi. A short while later a man in his early forties joined us in the hot tub and we began to talk. He told us he was vacationing with his wife and his two young children who were splashing about in the pool nearby.

"Where do you live?" I asked.

"In southern California."

"What kind of work do you do?"

"I'm a visual effects artist. I work for a visual effects company in Hollywood."

He gave me a list of some of the films he'd worked on. Several of them were horror films of the genre I refer to as shocker/slasher films.

"Those films contain some very disturbing images," I said.

"Yeah, I know. We help make those images."

He went on to talk about how much pressure there was to outdo previous films in the depiction of graphic violence.

"You can't create an effect that's already been done. It's got to be something new. For the film we just finished we had to show an eyeball exploding. It was complicated, but we eventually got it to work. It was very realistic. The director loved it."

"Have your kids watched any of these movies?" I asked.

"No," he said.

"Would you want them to see any of them?" I asked.

"No," he said, shaking his head. "Absolutely not."

I explained why we were at the hotel and how I was giving a talk the next morning about the entertainment industry. He seemed interested, even supportive.

So I said, "You're a creative artist. Why do you use your talent to work on films that you wouldn't want your own children to see?"

"Because I have to," he said.

"Why?"

"It's how Hollywood works. If you want the opportunity to work on good films, which is why I got into this business, then you have to work on the crappy films."

I didn't know what to say to this, and we sat for several seconds, the water swirling around us as his children's laughter echoed off the hard tiles surfaces.

"If we turn down a film," he continued, "they won't send us any more. So you have to take whatever comes along."

I recalled this conversation the next day as I gave my talk, and many times since. There was nothing cynical or callous in the man's comments. If anything, he was distressed by what he had to do. He clearly loved his children, and I suspect all children. He did not want to harm them. And yet I do not think, until that moment, he had really connected the dots. He loved films. He wanted to help make great films. Most artists would in this day and age. Sadly, however, he had convinced himself that to do the one, work on a great film, he had to do the other, spend weeks drawing upon his creative powers to make an eyeball explode in the most alarming way possible.

I am opposed to artistic censorship. But I also see that we have choices. We can refuse to watch certain kinds of films. We can even try and convince our children not watch these films, but that is never a sure bet. In my mother's day, a film played for week or two in the theaters and that was that. When I was a kid, a film might get a second life on television. But there were only three networks, and they were relatively circumspect when it came to the kind of films they broadcast. Today, with hundreds of cable stations, DVD rental companies, and on-demand services, a film lives forever. If those who possess creative talent, the writers, directors, cinematographers, actors, lighting grips, set designers, and special effect artists, are willing to make any kind of film, then all sorts of content, good and bad, flood the culture. The same principle applies to those who work in politics in this increasingly *mythos*-knowing age. What happens to society, for instance, when an experienced political consultant knows in his heart that a particular candidate is not up to the task of being governor, senator, or president of the United States and yet goes ahead and uses his knowledge of the mechanism of persuasion to see to it that the candidate wins the election anyway? Is he not like the young father in the Jacuzzi?

I have always loved the quote, "Give me a country of good customs rather than good laws." If we do not want an outside force telling us what to do, then we must choose to regulate ourselves. This can be done individually and collectively and is the hallmark of true leadership—people taking responsibility for the kind of society they want to be part of.

I believe an example of this kind of leadership can be found in the controversy that surrounded the making of the first *Scream* film in 1996. Wes Craven is a filmmaker who spent most of his career producing, writing, and directing horror/slasher films beginning with *A Nightmare on Elm Street*, which grew into a series of seven films featuring the murderous antics of a demon-ghost with a grotesquely scarred face that goes by the name Freddy Krueger. A serial killer who was caught and burned to death by a group of outraged parents, Freddy now stalks the dreams of their children, murdering them with a leather glove, each finger sprouting a long, razor-sharp blade.

Scream was Craven's first horror/slasher film after the *Nightmare* series. It begins with a high school student named Casey, played by the actress Drew Barrymore, who is brutally murdered by a ghost-masked figure wielding a butcher knife. Her parents arrive home moments later to find their only child has been hung from a tree like a gutted deer, her stomach slashed open.

The high school principal, Mr. Himbry, played by Henry Winkler of *Happy Days* fame, pretends to love young people but secretly hates them. A constant theme in Craven's films is the stupidity, duplicity, and hypocrisy of adult authority figures: doctors, nurses, teachers, and social workers are singled out for his most intense vitriolic scorn. Thus, when Himbry catches two students running down the hallway wearing ghost masks identical to the one worn by the murderer, he hauls them into his office.

"I'm sickened," he snarls as he rips off their masks. "Your whole havoc-inducing, thieving, whoring generation disgusts me. Two students have been savagely murdered. And this is how we express our compassion and sensitivity? We throw on a mask and dance around campus just hoping someone else gets butchered before we get bored again. You're both expelled."

The castigated students begin to whine, insisting that the punishment is not fair.

"No, it's not fair," Himbry snarls. "Fairness would be to rip your insides out and hang you from a tree so you can be exposed for the desensitized, heartless little shits that you are."

Later, however, when Himbry is alone in his office, he puts on one of the masks and begins to preen in front of a mirror, making scary gestures and uttering ghoulish noises. That, of course, is when the real ghost-masked murderer looms up from behind and stabs him in the back.

Other murders follow, one student has her head crushed by an automatic garage door, but the police fail to discover the killer's identity. That is because, as they eventually discover, there are *two* murderers working together. Nor are they adults as the police suspect, but fellow high school students. One has a grudge against the heroine's father and wants to frame him for the crimes. The other blames his actions on "peer pressure."

Kevin Williamson wrote the script for *Scream* and its sequels. What producer and director Wes Craven needed was just the right high school in which to shoot his film. It had to be located in an upscale, predominantly white community and have that "special" cinematic, classic retro quality he was looking for. He eventually decided that Santa Rosa High School in picturesque, film-friendly Sonoma County just north of San Francisco was the perfect location. The school had already made it into the movies back in 1986 when Frances Ford Coppola filmed *Peggy Sue Gets Married* on its campus.

Craven offered the school district $30,000 to rent the school and everything was fine and dandy until the contract went before the school board for approval. Unfortunately for Craven and his production company, Frightmare, Inc., and Miramax, the film's distributor, two women on the school board got hold of the script beforehand and were appalled by what they read. They lobbied the other school board members to put the kibosh on Craven's plans to use the school, and, in the end, the board voted four to one to turn down the request. The reason they gave publicly, however, following the advice of their *logos*-knowing attorney, was that the filming would be too disruptive to the proper functioning of the school.

This clearly was not what Wes Craven wanted to hear. Did they not realize he was an educator too? He earned his master's degree in writing and philosophy from John Hopkins University, taught college for several years, and even worked a year as a high school teacher before abandoning that confining, *logos*-knowing world to seek his fame and fortune in the more lucrative *mythos*-knowing world of filmmaking.

So he threatened to take the school district to court, claiming the principal of the high school verbally agreed to rent him the facility, an assertion the principal denied. He also complained about the expenses his film company incurred preparing for the shoot. Craven even reached out to the community for support and managed to convince the governor of California and the state's film commission to pressure the school district into allowing the filmmaker access to the campus. The school board realized that the potential cost to the district of defending against a major lawsuit could reach into the hundreds of thousands of dollars. Everyone's nerves were on edge, and a public hearing was scheduled by the school board that drew eight hundred people, with over a hundred parents, teachers, business owners, and film industry representatives speaking in favor or against the proposal.

In the end, the district held its ground and Craven, following the advice of a publicity team that feared the whole affair would give him and the movie a black eye, dropped the idea of a suit, renting instead the Sonoma Community Center, which he remodeled to look like a high school. But he was still angry with the school board for its refusal to acknowledge him as part of the new ruling class; he was, after all, a bishop in good standing of the new religion.

I was living in Northern California at the time and was fascinated by the issues the school rental controversy brought to light. Rather than censorship, I saw a community making a decision not to enable the telling of a story that was at odds with its own social norms. They did not want to promulgate images of their young people being cut to pieces by maniacs, nor did they want their children portrayed as murderous monsters or their principal as a jerk and a phony.

So I watched the film when it came out on video, wanting to see for myself what all the fuss was about. Craven insisted all along that the movie was in essence a dark comedy, a send-up of the horror/slasher genre. A sophisticated viewer was supposed to know all this and dismiss the murder and mayhem with a wry smile and a chuckle. All the same, I felt I had invited demons into my home as I watched the film. There was nothing "camp" in Barrymore's performance of a girl being repeatedly stabbed as she drags herself along the ground trailing a river of blood toward the sound of her parents' voices as they get out of their car, trying but unable to call out to them for help—an ironic twist on the film's title, I guess. Or later when the two murderers, in order to deflect police suspicion from themselves, begin stabbing each other only to get carried away by the blood lust and cut so deeply that one of them eventually dies.

I thought of the legions of young people who would watch these films, but lacking the filters of ironic sophistication, would miss the joke. Instead, through the powerful *mythos*-knowing technology of film, these images would penetrate to the deepest subterranean chambers of their psyches to pollute the springs of joy and hope that flow forth from those sacred places.

Then, as the ending credits rolled, I could hardly believe my eyes. In the section where the organizations that helped make the film possible were thanked—the city of Healdsburg, the Sonoma County Film Commission, etcetera—there appeared the following sentence:

"And no thanks at all to the Santa Rosa City School District."

It is a decisive *mythos*-knowing excommunication; as if Craven is saying, "Fail to kiss my ring, well, we'll see about that."

By the way, *Scream I*, released in December of 1996, earned over $170 million at the box office for Craven and company. *Entertainment Weekly* placed it at number thirty-two on its list of the fifty best high school films of all time.[32]

Before we leave the subject of Wes Craven, let's explore his views regarding the art and practice of storytelling. I have no personal vendetta against the man, but his movies are, I believe, symptomatic of a kind of hubris infecting a number of our new mythmakers.

In his last Freddy Krueger film, *The New Nightmare*, Craven plays himself. The plot revolves around the actress Heather Langenkamp, who played the protagonist Nancy in the first *Nightmare on Elm Street* film. In *The New Nightmare*, we are led to believe that we are watching Heather go about her life in the real world. She is a working actress in Los Angeles, her husband is a special effects artist for a film studio, and she has a six-year-old son named Dylan who begins having nightmares about Freddy. As in the other films, Freddy begins to step out of the child's nightmares into the world of here and now, where he kills the boy's father and, later, his much beloved baby-

---

32. Many adults are unfamiliar with these kinds of films. They are effectively "under the radar." But their sons and daughters, their nephews and nieces, their granddaughter and grandsons know all about them. Not only do the films live for a season in the movie theaters, they continue forever like zombies on DVDs and through the on-demand service of cable companies, making it nearly impossible for a young person to avoid watching them at some point.

sitter. This second murder occurs in a hospital room where Freddy stabs the innocent girl with his long, glistening-sharp knives and then lifts her into the air and drags her up the wall and across the ceiling, her blood dripping down on the white linoleum floor. She cannot see Freddy, but the young Dylan can, and so she reaches her hand toward the little boy, her face a mask of pain, terror, and desperation, as she weakly implores, "Help me."

But all Dylan can do is cry out her name as Freddy, standing upside down, his feet on the ceiling, cocks his head to one side, curls the knives of his other hand into a fist, and purrs to the boy, "Ever play skin the cat?"

The demon lets loose a diabolical laugh and snaps the girl's neck. She falls lifeless to the floor as Dylan lets out a scream of utter despair.

In the next scene, Heather drives out to see Wes at his mansion in the hills overlooking the city. Wes, playing himself, tells Heather about a nightmare he has been having and how, each morning when he gets up, he writes it down, and it is becoming the movie that, clever boy that he is, we are now watching projected on the screen.

Then, as a spokesman for his genre, he provides a description of what storytellers do for children:

> **Wes**: *I wish I could tell you where this script is going, Heather, but the fact is I don't know. I dream a scene at night and write it down in the morning. Beyond that, your guess is as good as mine where it's going.*
>
> **Heather**: *At least tell me what it's about so far?*
>
> **Wes**: *I can tell you what the nightmare is so far. It's about this entity, whatever you want to call it, it's old, it's very old. It's existed in different forms in different times. About the only thing about it that stays the same is what it lives for, really.*

Heather: *What's that?*

Wes: *The murder of innocence.*

Heather: *This is still a script we're talking about, right, Wes?*

Wes: *Yeah, well, I think of it as a nightmare in progress.*

Heather: *Well in this nightmare in progress, does this thing have any weakness?*

Wes: *Well, it can be captured sometimes.*

Heather: *Captured? How?*

Wes: *By storytellers, of all things. Every so often they imagine a story good enough to sort of catch its essence. And then for a while it's held prisoner in the story.*

Heather: *Like the genie in the bottle.*

Wes: *Exactly. But the problem comes when the story dies, and that can happen in a lot of ways: it can get too familiar to people, or somebody waters it down to make it an easier sell, you know, or maybe it's just so upsetting to society that it's banned outright. However it happens, when the story dies, the evil is set free.*

Heather: *You're saying Freddy, this ancient thing—*

Wes: *Right. Current version. And for ten years he's been held captive pretty much as Freddy in the Nightmare on Elm Street series. But now that the films have ended, the genie's out of the bottle. That's what the nightmares are telling me and that's what I'm writing.*

Heather: *Well, if Freddy is loose in your script, where's he going to go? Another age? Another form?*

Wes: *No, that's not what the dreams have him doing, though.*

Heather: *What is he doing?*

Wes: *Well, you see, he's sort of got used to being Freddy now and he likes our time and space, so he's decided to cross over. Out of films, into our reality.*

Heather: *Isn't there somebody who can stop him?*

Wes: *Actually there is a person in the dreams, a gatekeeper so to speak, somebody Freddy has to get by before he can come through into our world. That person's you, Heather.*

Heather: *Why me?*

Wes: *Well dramatically speaking, it makes perfect sense. You played Nancy, after all, and you were the first to humiliate him, defeat him—*

Heather: *That was Nancy, Wes. Not me.*

Wes: *Yeah, but it was you who gave Nancy her strength. So in order to get out, he's got to come through you. And it's inevitable that he's going to try and do that at your most vulnerable points.*

Heather: *Oh my God, Wes. Did you know?* (fade in spooky music)

Wes: *(uncertain) It was a script. It was a dream. I didn't. . . I didn't—*

Heather: *You know damn well it's more than that now. Wes. . .Wes, how can we stop him?*

Wes: *I think the only way to stop him is to make another movie. And I swear to you I'm going to stay by this computer and keep writing until I complete the script. But when that time comes, you're going to have to make a choice.*

Heather: *Choice? What kind of choice?*

Wes: *Whether or not you're willing to play Nancy one last time.*

I believe it is fair to say Wes Craven launched a preemptive strike when he added this scene to his film. It allowed him to speak directly to his youth audience, to tell them that not only are his films harmless but as their storyteller, he is *protecting* them. It is Wes Craven, in other words, who is keeping the evil Freddy locked up in his stories—that is until the hypocritical, clueless do-gooders begin interfering and making matters much worse. For who are parents, educators, and health professionals if not the Mr. Himbrys of this world?

This is where content and medium comes together for me. I have watched a coarsening of the stories we tell our children over the years. When I ask adults why young people watch movies like *Scream*, *Halloween*, *Hellraiser*, and *Friday the Thirteenth*, the answer I invariable get is, "They just like to get scared."

And this is true; *mythos* knowing is about sensation, and these movies appeal to the senses. Yet, since the dawn of time, human beings have looked to stories to make sense of the world. Who among us does not occasionally wonder what comes after death? Does good win out in the end? Are there demons and angels? Do our actions in the physical world have any bearing on what takes place in the spirit world?

A reporter once asked Albert Einstein what he considered the most important question of all and Einstein replied: "Is the universe friendly?"

That is what we are all trying to figure out. Therefore, it should come as no surprise that our children are asking those same questions and seeking out those stories that purport to provide at least some of the answers. It is about more than getting an adrenaline rush. Inside the cineplex and from our wide-screen television sets at home, the dominant mythmaking "churches" of today, our children learn about ghosts and demons, about moral justice, or the lack of it. They learn that good wins out in the end, or that it does not, that life has meaning and a higher purpose or is merely a series of random, nonsensical events. They learn that innocence is a virtue or a serious liability and that you can protect yourself by being kind and good or that being kind and good has nothing to do with whether or not you will be cut to pieces; that, in fact, sometimes the terrors we experience in our dreams can climb out of those dreams into our waking world and harm those we love most.

* * *

I came across a 1930s recording of a song from a poem by C.C. Miller that often comes to mind when I think about the responsibility storytellers have for the stories they tell.

"Twas a sheep not a lamb that strayed away,
In the parable Jesus told.
Twas a grown-up sheep that wandered away,
From the ninety and nine in the fold.
Out on the hillside, out in the cold,
Twas a sheep the Good Shepherd sought.
And back to the flock, and safe in the fold,
Twas a sheep the Good Shepherd brought.
Now why must the sheep be so carefully fed and cared for still today,
Because there's danger if they go wrong,
They'll lead the lambs astray.
Because the lambs will follow the sheep, you know,
Wherever they wander, wherever they go,
And if the sheep go wrong, it won't be long,
Until the lambs are as wrong as they.
And so with the sheep we must earnestly plead,
For the sake of the lambs today;
Because if the lambs are lost, what a terrible cost,
Some sheep will have to pay.

CONCLUSION

The Sustainable Imagination

THERE IS IN ME SOMETHING OF THE HOARDER, but, instead of cramming my basement full of dusty *National Geographics* or tackle boxes stuffed with vintage fishing lures, I fill my mind with stories, and the older I get, the more I fill it with stories about how and why we tell stories.

When I was traveling the country recording people for my family stories radio series, I used to fret about all the great stories I failed to capture on tape. During an event at a public library or ethnic festival I would invite people to come forward and share a family story with the audience; now and again someone would tell a fascinating tale about how her grandmother Olga was hidden from the Nazis in an orphanage or how his Uncle Arlen carried a wildcat around town in a suitcase. But then the teller would vanish before I had a chance to schedule a time to record her story, and this regret of "the story that got away" often nagged me for days.

One afternoon, I wandered into a used bookstore in Chicago and came across a book published in 1937 with the title, *The American Book of Days*. The author was George Douglas, and the book was filled with odd bits of history and related folk customs for each day of the year, just the kind of book I like having in my library. But the most valuable part of the book, I later discovered, was a quote by Plato on the title page that read:

"As it is the commendation of a good huntsman to find game in the wild wood, so it is no imputation if he hath not caught all."

Thus instructed by Plato, I will bring this exploration of modern mythmaking to a close by returning to the legend of Perseus and Medusa.

Perseus has committed himself to slaying the gorgon Medusa. To do this, however, he finds he must first acquire three magical objects: a cap of invisibility, a pair of winged sandals, and a leather satchel that expands in size to hold whatever is placed inside. These objects are in the possession of certain nymphs who like nothing better than cavorting in a secret garden. To find the nymphs and their garden, Perseus must journey to the cave of the Graeae, three ancient witches who alone can tell him what he needs to know. The names of the witches are Deino, Enyo, and Pemphredo (Dread, Horror, and Alarm) and they are blind and are forced share a single eye, which they pass back and forth between them. So, employing great stealth, Perseus enters their cave and manages to snatch away the eye just as one witch is about to pass it to another. Holding the eye hostage, he orders the witches to tell him where he can find the secret garden of the nymphs. They tell him—they have no choice—but, instead of returning their precious eye, Perseus throws it into a lake, leaving the witches to wail in misery, forever blind.

When we switch on radio or television for the news these days, we find ourselves confronting the three Graeae—dread, horror, and alarm. And to the extent we limit our political and cultural discourse as a society to these *mythos*-heavy electronic mediums, we become more and more like the witches who have only one eye between them with which to perceive the world. What might happen if a corporation or political party were to take possession of that eye? Must we not, like the Graeae, do whatever the new owner of the eye demands: vote for a particular candidate, get rid of taxes and government regulation, expend our resources on wars in distant lands while our own cities crumble and we shutter our schools and libraries? I believe the potential for such compulsion is an important argument against the increasing amount of media consolidation we have witnessed in recent years. In the way living organisms in the natural world rely on diversity as a hedge against extinction, so human society should promote diversification in the number and variety of its storytelling mediums. Television does some things well, as does the Internet and film. But we still need newspapers and well thought-out books. We also need public venues where people can learn about and discuss the pressing issues of the day without fear of violence or other forms of retaliation.

One such venue is the public and school library. It is fair to say this book would not exist if not for the public library in my town, because the librarians provided me with a wealth of resources: books, films, magazine articles, and databases. Libraries are a essential part of the commons in an age when the commons are fast disappearing. They belong to all of us, and as with public education, public libraries are wrestling to find an appropriate balance between the demands of *logos* and *mythos* knowing. Libraries are not simply repositories of information, they are also complex social environments, welcoming all, excluding no one, rich and poor, young and old, assuring equal access to knowledge, protecting the principle of free speech—lively local institutions that are vital to our democratic way of life.

* * *

A reason to limit our exposure to electronic media came to me one day while I was driving through farm country in the Midwest. I noticed a massive tractor moving slowly across a vast soybean field. The tractor was towing a chemical tank with a spray rack suspended behind. My guess was that the farmer was applying fertilizer made from petrochemicals onto his field in hopes of increasing the yield.

We can use this farming metaphor to better appreciate the kind of industrialized storytelling we have today, a storytelling that is standardized and commodified, electronically created, enhanced, and distributed.

Compare that part of ourselves we call the imagination with the soil of a farmer's field, but instead of growing soybeans, this soil grows fantasy, dreams, and creative ideas. Without a flash of fantasy now and again, life loses its zest and zeal. We fantasize a better future for ourselves and our children, one that will give us the determination to push through the difficulties and heartaches of life. We fantasize about romantic love in hopes of keeping it fresh and meaningful.

Dreams too are vitally important. A fascinating discovery that springs from sleep research is that we must dream to stay healthy. When subjects in sleep experiments were woken up every time they went into the dream state, indicated by REM, rapid eye movement, they became increasingly agitated when awake. After only a few days of not dreaming, they began to hallucinate, to become delusional, their behavior erratic and paranoid. But once they were allowed to dream again without interruption, these symptoms disappeared.

This does not answer the question of *why* we dream, it only tells us that we *must* dream to stay mentally fit. And because our fantasies and dreams arise from our imaginations, we must see to it that our imaginations are properly fertilized in much the same way that the farmer must fertilize his field. That is where entertainment enters the picture. For some the word "entertainment" is synonymous with triviality, a pleasant but essentially meaningless waste of time. But if by "entertainment" we mean the enjoyment of stories, songs, images, and play, then we are talking about something fundamental, because these experiences stimulate and renew our imaginations.

The problem with industrial forms of entertainment, and television news coverage often falls into this category, is they increasingly over-stimulate our imaginations with what entertainment executives refer to as "jolts per minute," in the way petrochemicals over-stimulate the soil, exhausting it over time. Even when we consume what we consider to be quality electronic entertainment, an Academy award-winning film, for instance, or an Emmy-winning HBO series, or the newest hip commercial, the net result is the same. Communication technologies can and do evolve rapidly, but the evolution of the imagination, which is tied to the biological functioning of our brains, takes much longer.

As a nation, we face threats from multiple directions including terrorism, climate change, financial instability, overpopulation, and viral and bacterial pandemics; and yet, we seem unable to come up with creative and workable responses to these challenges. Politicians and government bureaucrats are not necessarily more corrupt and less intelligent than the rest of us, despite what some of the cable news channels would have us believe. Their imaginations are simply overwhelmed by the constant input of the 24/7 news/entertainment industrial complex. I would go further and say our collective imagination is exhausted because stimulation begets stimulation; we are caught in a kind of technologically-driven addiction. Therefore I believe we should explore the concept of a sustainable imagination, explore what goes into maintaining a sustainable and healthy imagination. Reading a book, painting a picture, playing a musical instrument, memorizing a poem, planting tomatoes, restoring a wooden canoe, knitting a scarf, learning to tango, going fishing, sewing a dress, hosting a dinner party, even flying a kite, activities that by today's standards may be regarded as quaint pastimes, are the very nutrients the imagination needs to live and to thrive. That is why they have lasted so long; they work.

I have already mentioned how electronic journalists and political pundits, traditionally regarded as members of the fourth estate, are taking over the authority and prerogatives of the first estate to become the new priests of our society. I had a powerful experience a few years ago that brought this reality home to me.

For some time, I have been working on a project entitled *Among the Storytellers*. It is a Studs Terkel-style oral history of working storytellers including interviews not only with those we naturally think of as storytellers: novelists, filmmakers, playwrights, humorists, and journalists, but also with trial attorneys, preachers, museum exhibit designers, advertising executives, military commanders, news photographers, politicians, even astrologers and tattoo artists—in other words, anyone who uses stories in one way or another as an integral part of the work they do in the world.

One person I wished to interview for this project was Judge Andrew Napolitano who served for eight years as a superior court judge for the state of New Jersey. He subsequently left the bench to become an on-air political and legal analyst for FOX News. Besides hosting his own program on the network, he regularly appeared on *The O'Reilly Factor* and filled in as host for Glenn Beck when that worthy was off somewhere causing civil mischief.

I called his office, and we set up the interview to coincide with a visit I was making to New York City.

"He'll meet you at the News Corp Building in Manhattan and you can do the interview there," his personal secretary, a pleasant woman, informed me. Then, on the day before my flight to New York, she called again.

"The Judge wanted me to tell you that FOX News does not permit interviews to be recorded. I hope that's not a problem."

For a moment I was speechless. It seemed foolhardy of me to interview someone from FOX News, or any major corporation for that matter, without having a recording of the interview.

I worried that if the Judge did indeed say something that the spin doctors at FOX didn't like, especially as I hoped to talk about the ethics of storytelling, then I would need the recording to defend myself should FOX decide to sue me or my publisher. So, it was either get permission to record the interview or cancel. I pleaded my case to the secretary, whom I sensed was sympathetic to my position.

"Let me see if anything can be done," she said and called back an hour later with the happy news: the Judge would allow the recording after all.

My first order of business in New York was to meet with a literary agent in Greenwich Village, after which I took the subway uptown to Rockefeller Center. I had an hour to spare before my interview with Judge Napolitano, and I decided to find a restaurant and grab some lunch. As I walked down the street between the skyscrapers, a thin strip of blue above me, I passed the headquarters for CNN, HBO, NBC, McGraw-Hill, and others of our nation's largest media conglomerates, all clustered together in a dozen or so blocks between Rockefeller Center and Times Square. Eventually, I came upon a small sandwich shop near the corner of 49th Street and 7th Avenue, and, after ordering a grilled turkey panini, I found a seat at the counter that looked out onto the street. Directly across from me was the global headquarters for the investment-banking firm Lehman Brothers. The building was an imposing thirty-two-floor office tower, with the first six floors serving as one massive television screen. Alternating images of thundering waterfalls, majestic mountain ranges, and spectacular scarlet-hued sunsets appeared on the 49th Street side of the building and scrolled around the corner to continue down 7th Avenue. It was quite an eyeful, and, as I thought about all the media companies in that part of the city, a strange idea came to me: if the entire planet was a single human body with the different countries and cities its different organs, then I was sitting inside the brain of that body. Not only that, but I was inside the part of the brain where images were created, the synapses crackling as electric currents pulsed through miles of nerve-like fiber optic cables. It was a kind of goosebumps moment, and, as I lifted my sandwich to take a bite, I noticed that the parading images on the Lehman Brothers Headquarters had been replaced by words that marched from right to left across the side of the building. The first set of words were, not surprisingly, LEHMAN BROTHERS. But then came another group, the letters ten feet high: WHERE VISION GETS BUILT.

I nearly choked; it was exactly what I was thinking and feeling.

Twenty minutes later, I was standing on the west side of 5th Avenue across the street from the News Corp Building, a welter of shiny steel and glass reaching up into the Manhattan sky. Filling the spacious plaza in front of the building's entrance was an enormous crowd. I thought at first it was an anti-FOX News protest, but as I crossed the street and drew closer, I saw that the people were in a festive mood, everyone smiling and talking excitedly. Moving among them was a cadre of men dressed in bright orange jump suits, each with a set of police handcuffs dangling from a wrist as he handed out cards of some sort to passersby. One even came up to me and handed me a card. It resembled the joker from a deck of playing cards, with the image of the horned, goateed devil leering up at me surrounded by gambling dice, gold coins, and a four leaf clover. It took me a moment to realize that the card was, in fact, a temporary rub-on tattoo. I also noticed that there were lines of people in front of tables where tattoo artists were giving away free permanent tattoos to anyone who wanted one, courtesy of the FOX Television Network. It was all part of a promotion for a new FOX television series called *Prison Break*.

I tried to imagine someone strolling by, a secretary, perhaps, on her lunch break, or a couple of tourists from Topeka, who decide on the spur of the moment to get a tattoo. I was tempted to get in line for one of the tables to see what tattoos designs were being offered? Did they all relate to the television series in some way? But then I gazed upon the News Corp Building, proud and serene, like some medieval cathedral, on the far side of this crowded carnival and I knew I had no time to dally. Back in the good old days of the fourteenth century, when the spires of Notre Dame, Chartres, and Salisbury dominated the urban landscape, the broad plazas in front of cathedrals provided the setting for the pursuit of earthly delights, the buying and selling of livestock and sexual favors, money lending, performances by itinerant puppeteers and jugglers, the odd freak shows. Thus the cathedral precinct was very often a place of extremes, the profane and the sacred cheek by jowl. Or so it seemed to me in New York City on that afternoon, surrounded by pretend convicts and busy tattoo needles—pickpockets and con men, too, for all I knew—as I prepared to enter the media temple.

Another "convict" accosted me as I thread my way through the crowd. "Don't you want a real tattoo?" he asked.

"No," I said. "Thanks."

At last, I reached the entrance and passed through the revolving glass door. I had to check in at a long, sleek security counter, behind which sat a half dozen security guards dressed in matching blue sports blazers, their faces bathed in the soft glow of computer monitors hidden below the granite counter top. To their left was a pair of security portals/metal detectors with opposing steel panels like the jaws of a great beast, that slid open and closed at the push of a button allowing people to enter or leave the building's inner sanctum. It was spookily quiet inside the security area compared with the ruckus outside, and, as I handed over my driver's license and business card, I thought of the Vatican and the Swiss guards whose avowed job it was to protect the worthies inside. These modern security guards looked just as dedicated, though they lacked the colorful uniforms and tall pikes, and despite my attempts to elicit a smile, I was vetted with stony efficiency.

Soon, a discreetly dressed, soft-spoken young woman appeared like a lowly priest in black cassock to lead me upstairs into the presence of His Eminence.

"I'm an assistant producer," she told me as we rode the elevator to one of the upper floors, where she led me down a hallway to a conference room right next to another room with the word "payroll" on the door.

"You can set up for your interview in here," she said. "The Judge will be with you in a few minutes."

I thanked her and proceeded to set up my gear.

The judge entered, we shook hands, and he sat down across the table from me.

"What did you think of my new book?" he asked.

An unfortunate start, I thought.

"I'm sorry," I said, "I never read it."

He looked confused and slightly irritated.

"I want to interview you about the work you do here at FOX News," I said.

He looked at his watch in a manner that made me half-expect him to call off the interview.

"My brother went to Seton Hall Law School," I added, having read that Judge Napolitano had once taught a course there. "He practices insurance law in New Jersey."

This changed the mood in the room.

"That's a good school," the judge said with a smile, and from that moment on he was fully engaged. We talked about his parents, who immigrated to the United States from Italy in the early part of the twentieth century. They were great fans of the Italian nationalist hero Giuseppe Garibaldi and fervent supporters of Franklin Delano Roosevelt and the New Deal. Napolitano then talked about attending Princeton, where he studied history, and Notre Dame, where he earned his law degree. Afterwards, he went into private practice until he was appointed a judge, the youngest lifetime tenured judge in New Jersey.

"So why did you leave the bench?" I asked.

"I was tired of being poor and needed to make some money," he said with something of a chuckle. "I mean, judges in the federal system are not allowed any earned outside income in excess of twenty percent of their base income."

That meant no fat speaking fees or consultancies. So he resigned his judicial post and called a press conference to explain why. This caught the attention of the head of CNBC who called him to ask if he would consider serving as an on-air analyst for the O.J. Simpson trial. The head of CNBC, as it happens, was Roger Ailes, the brilliant political consultant who helped get a number of Republicans elected president. Rupert Murdock later tapped Ailes to head up the FOX News division, and Ailes asked Judge Napolitano to join the FOX News team as well.

But I believe the most significant part of the interview was when I asked the judge if he ever worried or lost sleep about the legal opinions he broadcast to millions of viewers.

"I don't anguish over phrases and I usually don't even prepare phrases ahead of time. We have been taught by the great Roger Ailes, who is a master with words. Before he ran the FOX News Channel, he was advising everybody from Ronald Reagan to Richard Nixon to George H. W. Bush to the CEOs of Fortune 100 corporations on how to use words, how to convey ideas. One of the things that Roger has taught us—especially in my end of the work, and by my end I mean as the person who is usually answering, as opposed to asking, the questions on air— one of the things that Roger Ailes has taught us is that your initial response is usually your best. Not only is it usually your most intellectually honest, but it's usually your best choice of words. So even when I'm interviewed by our anchors—we all know what I'm going to talk about—they want to induce me to explain some aspect of the law. And even though I have an idea what questions are going to come to me, I do not prepare answers. I want my answers to be truly spontaneous, because they are more likely than not to be the best answers with the best choice of words."

Having thought about *mythos* and *logos* knowing a great deal over the years, I understood what he was saying. Television is a *mythos*-knowing medium; it thrives on spontaneity. Roger Ailes understands this, and the judge, after having endured the *logos*-knowing rigors of Princeton and Notre Dame along with eight more years as a judge slogging his way through untold numbers of legal briefs and transcribed testimony, was apparently willing to set aside this *logos*-knowing training and experience so he could sit at the feet of the master, who would initiate him

into the marvels and delights of the new consciousness. Judge
Napolitano had learned his lessons well and was now a bishop of
the new religion in his own right, an honest-to-God television
personality.

But if spontaneity makes for first-rate, engaging television,
does it also further meaningful civic discourse? I have my
doubts.

All the same, I could not help liking Judge Napolitano. He
was friendly, sincere, and brimming with energy. Even though
he obviously had rejected the liberal political views of his
immigrant parents, he spoke of them with genuine affection.

Before I knew it an hour had passed and the Judge looked at
his watch and suddenly stood.

"We've got to wrap this up," he said with some alarm, "I'm
on the air in five minutes."

"Well, I think I have what I came for. Your assistant can take
me downstairs if you have to go," I said.

"She's not available," the Judge said, again looking at his
watch, "I've got to take you downstairs myself."

I was tempted to say, "I can show myself out," but I knew
this was impossible. It would be like wandering around inside
the Vatican without a handler—too many secrets lying about.
Just ask Dan Brown.

So I hurriedly disconnected the microphone, headphones,
and recorder. I then flung my bag over my shoulder and we
hurried to the elevator.

When we reached the first floor, the Judge escorted me to
the security portal and motioned to a guard who sat behind a
bulletproof window to open the panels. The judge then took
my hand, and as he shook it, he looked me in the eye and said,
"God bless you, Joe."

In his tone of voice, in the gentle but firm grasp of his hand,
in his whole demeanor, he was suddenly Pat O'Brien in the

film *Angels With Dirty Faces*, or perhaps Bing Crosby as Father O'Malley in *Going My Way*.

Then he turned and hurried back to the elevator where in the twinkle of an eye his image and voice would go out over the airwaves, while I pushed my way through the revolving door of the News Corp Building to rejoin the free-tattoo, media-driven craziness that is our world today.

ACKNOWLEDGMENTS

I am grateful for the help I received from my wife Paula and daughters Anna and Emily. I would also like to thank the following individuals and organizations: Mack Armstrong, Thomas P.M. Barnett, Judy Bushell, Jeanie Murphy, Pete Seeger, Sarita Schaffer, Patrick McHugh, Clara McHugh, Georganna Carey-Galateau, Angus Heriot, Terry Setter, Rev. Amy Walters, Sherrie and Larry Fisher, Barbara Reynolds, Connie Williams, Kathy Green, Gene Hoover, Rebecca Bossen, Fr. Joe Kramis, Joanna Robinson, Bruce "Utah" Phillips, Karen Ostrov, Fr. Jan Larson, Pat Krafcik, John Noakes, Dr. Dan Ben-Amos, Carol Piening, and the generous folks at First Christian Church in Olympia, Washington.

About the Author

JOE MCHUGH is a storyteller, public radio producer, and old-time fiddler who lectures nationally on the art and practice of storytelling in the modern age. He has authored two collections of American folktales and humor and an illustrated children's book about the early days of aviation. His novel *Kilowatt* explores the perils of energy capitalism and the sacredness of time.

To learn more about his work, please visit:

www.americanfamilystories.org
www.joemchugh.info
www.callingcrane.com